The Compleat
Day Trader II

Library of Congress Cataloging-in-Publication Data

Bernstein, Jacob, date.
    The compleat day trader II / by Jake Bernstein.
        p.   cm.
    Continues: The compleat day trader.
    ISBN 0-07-094501-2
    1. Futures. 2. Futures market. I. Bernstein, Jacob, date.
Compleat day trader. II. Title.
HG6024.A3B478   1998
332.64'5—dc21   98-5656
                                              CIP

McGraw-Hill

A Division of The McGraw·Hill Companies

1 2 3 4 5 6 7 8 9 10 DOC/DOC 9 0 3 2 1 0 9 8

ISBN 0-07-094501-2

The sponsoring editor for this book was Stephen Isaacs, the editing supervisor was Caroline R. Levine, and the production supervisor was Suzanne W. B. Rapcavage. This book was set in Palatino by Victoria Khavkina of McGraw-Hill's Professional Book Group composition unit.

Printed and bound by R. R. Donnelley & Sons Company.

This book is printed on recycled, acid-free paper containing a minimum of 50% recycled, de-inked fiber.

The Compleat
Day Trader II

Jake Bernstein

McGraw-Hill

New York   San Francisco   Washington, D.C.   Auckland   Bogotá
Caracas   Lisbon   London   Madrid   Mexico City   Milan
Montreal   New Delhi   San Juan   Singapore
Sydney   Tokyo   Toronto

Contents

Preface

When I wrote *The Compleat Day Trader* in 1995, I felt that the science and art of day trading had come of age. Given the increased price volatility and technological advances in the delivery and analysis of market-related data, it was clear to me that there would be numerous opportunities for the day trader. And this has indeed been the case. Yet the other side of opportunity is risk. With increased potential for profit comes increased potential for loss. My sense of the markets is that more traders than ever before are either day trading or have a desire to day trade. Do not, however, confuse or equate an increase in the number of day traders with an increase in the percentage of traders who actually win at this high stakes game. I believe that day traders and aspiring day traders need more effective tools to help them navigate the ever more treacherous market waters. My goals, therefore, in writing this new book on day trading were as follows:

- To present and discuss some of my latest day-trading systems and methods
- To share new ideas and to amplify on existing ideas for effective risk management both from the standpoint of market methodology and trader psychology
- To suggest new and promising directions in day trading techniques
- To fine-tune techniques and methods I have previously discussed

I believe that I have exceeded my original goals. I believe that this book offers several powerful tools as well as numerous promising concepts for further exploration.

The book you are about to read contains a variety of different methods and systems for day trading. Take the time to learn, study, and track the methods. Then, after you have learned the techniques that appeal to your senses and your pocketbook, begin trading with them. But don't plunge into the markets before you have spent some time learning the methods. And when you start your trading, please make certain you understand the risks as well as the rewards of day trading. Be certain to start with sufficient capital and practice all the necessary discipline your methods require.

Finally, do not labor under the misconception that day trading is easy. Although there are several distinct advantages to day trading, it may be true that from the standpoint of self-discipline, day trading is more difficult than position trading. You cannot day trade your way to riches with little effort. Day trading takes work, work, and more work. It requires discipline, attention, organization, and commitment. Success as a day trader does not fall out of a magazine or a book.

I hope that the tools in this book and in my *Compleat Day Trader* will help you, and I wish you success in your venture. If I can be of assistance, please contact me at the following address:

jake@trade-futures.com

For new developments in my day-trading research visit the following Internet location:

http://www.trade-futures.com

Jake Bernstein
Northbrook, Illinois

Acknowledgments

The amount of research that went into the production of this book was enormous. Without the assistance of system-testing software and valid historical data my task would have been impossible to complete. Accordingly, I wish to extend thanks to the following individuals, firms, and organizations for their valuable assistance:

- Commodity Quote Graphics of Glenwood Springs, Colorado, for permission to reprint charts from SYSTEM ONE, their outstanding quotation/graphics hardware and software program. The CQG software is especially useful in day trading. It has been one of my most valuable day-trading tools for many years and it continues to serve me well.

- Mr. Bill Cruz of Omega Research in Miami, Florida, and his excellent staff for their continuing assistance and for permission to use reports generated by their excellent system testing software program, TradeStation™. This highly developed and advanced program makes the intensive task of historical testing and system development effective and efficient. It is well-suited to the needs of all day traders.

- Mr. Glen Larson of Genesis Financial Data is due many thanks for his constant supply of historical daily and tick-by-tick data. The development, evaluation, and testing of day-trading systems, indicators, and methods are impossible without accurate tick-by-tick data.

- FutureSource is due a word of thanks for permission to reproduce charts from their excellent trading software.

- I am also thankful to all traders who have touched my life with their opinions, suggestions, systems, methods, and timing indicators.

- My dedicated and hard-working office staff are also commended for their persistent efforts in the production of this book. I am not easy to work with. I change my mind too easily and too quickly although all turns out well in the long run.

- And finally, many thanks to my family for their patience and willingness to give me the time I needed to complete this important project.

Jake Bernstein

The Compleat
Day Trader II

1

A Perspective on Day Trading

Observations, Claims, and Caveats

Beware that you do not lose the substance by grasping at the shadow.

AESOP

Now more than ever, day trading is both a viable as well as a potentially profitable venture that is open and available to all traders. While day trading was once the fiercely guarded and virtually exclusive domain of the professional trader, significant advances in the speed of communications and in computer technology have made it possible for the average trader to participate in and to win at what I consider to be "the fastest game in town." No longer does the floor trader have exclusive rights to the spoils of day trading. Virtually any trader, armed with knowledge, a trading system or method, and sufficient starting capital can compete effectively in this high stakes game.

However, the possibility of profitable day trading is nothing more than an unattainable dream if the rules and procedures of the game are not properly understood, learned, and applied. It is the rare individual indeed who is capable of achieving the discipline and persistence that are among the prerequisites for success as a day trader.

In order to achieve this end, the following inputs and ingredients must be present (not necessarily in order of importance):

- Knowledge of trading terms, methods, systems, and indicators
- Sufficient starting capital, all of which must be risk capital
- One or more viable, tested, effective, and operational trading systems, methods, and/or indicators
- The time, patience, and persistence to effectively and consistently implement the indicators, systems, and/or methods
- The discipline to follow through on trading signals
- The discipline to take losses and profits when so indicated by the system or method being used for day trading

I will dispense with preliminary definitions and explanations rather quickly. This book is intended for traders who already have an understanding of the markets and of trading basics. Experience in trading would also be helpful. Therefore, please do not consider my cursory treatment of any subject herein to be a denigration of its importance. It is merely an indication that the information is either too basic or that it has been discussed in my other books. For those seeking an introductory text on day trading, please note that the basics of day trading have already been discussed in my book *The Compleat Day Trader* (1995). This book provides a thorough examination of day trading rules, procedures, and basic principles, as well as several trading systems or methods.

Why Day Trade?

If you plan to take the time, energy, and effort to day trade, it would be a good idea to know why. The mere attraction or sex appeal of day trading is insufficient reason to get involved in this intensive, frequently time-consuming, and potentially costly venture. The most obvious answer to the basic question "why day trade?" is "to make money." But the motivation to trade is not often simple. In order to day trade profitably, it is important to first understand and acknowledge what motivation, if any, exists above and beyond the simple profit incentive.

Given my own extensive experience in day trading, as well as my observation of other day traders over the years, here are some thoughts about why one might want to consider day trading:

The Profit Potential.   This is clearly the most obvious reason. Given the wide market swings that are now commonplace in many of the futures markets, both domestic and foreign, many opportunities are available within the time frame of a single trading day. In addition to the wide price swings, the intraday market trends are often persistent. By this I mean that once a market trend begins within a given day, that trend tends to persist. Clearly this is not always the case. Market trends can and do reverse within the time frame of a day, but there are systems, methods, and procedures by which the day trader can take advantage of such changes or, at the very least, protect his or her position when such changes in trend occur.

In S&P 500 futures, the quintessential day traders' market, price swings of over 1000 points within the day time frame are relatively commonplace. This is a $2500 trading range, which is certainly large enough for the day trader. Figure 1-1 shows a daily price chart of S&P 500 futures for the period from October through

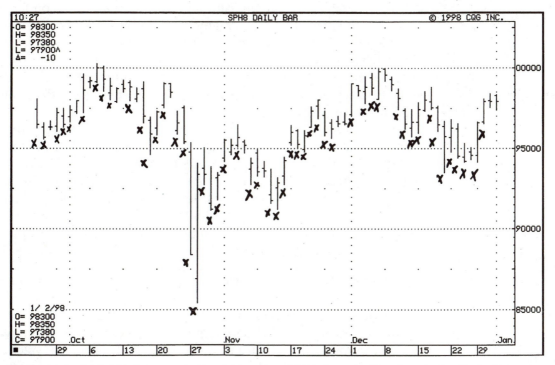

Figure 1-1. S&P 500 futures October–December 1997 showing days (marked "X") of 1000-point range or larger.

December 1997. I have marked an "X" by each day that had a trading range of 1000 points or more. As you can see, there were many such days, all of which provided ample and potentially profitable opportunities for the day trader.

Large daily trading ranges also occur regularly in Treasury bond, coffee, Swiss franc, British pound, and Japanese yen futures. The petroleum futures markets have also had large daily trading ranges but with less frequency than the markets cited above. In addition to these markets, a number of European futures markets have had large daily trading ranges. Hence, the opportunities for day trading exist in many different markets both domestically and abroad.

Naturally, where there exists the opportunity for profit, there is also the risk of loss. Even the least experienced trader understands that there is a risk of loss, but it is imperative that I underscore this risk lest any readers conclude that day trading somehow involves less risk than position trading.

The Challenge.   Yet another very viable reason for day trading is the challenge of the game. Although this is clearly a secondary motive to the profit incentive, many of us derive considerable personal satisfaction from a venture that can both make us money and satisfy an intellectual or competitive need at the same time. When a trader is new to the markets, the main goal is survival with the hope of profit. Once the game has been learned, the goal is profit as well as mastery.

The challenge of successful day trading is one that has lured many a trader over the years. And many traders have been left in the ashes of ruin as a consequence of playing the game with faulty tools or without discipline. Therefore, to a given extent, the ability to day trade profitably with consistency is a measure both of an individual's ability to understand the markets and to develop profitable tools based on these understandings, and then to put these understandings into action.

The Fame.   The lure of fame cannot be ignored as one of the reasons traders undertake day trading as either a hobby or as a profession. Hopefully, the ego of the trader as well as the need for fame will not overshadow the desire to make a profit. But fame as a day trader cannot be achieved without profitable trading or system development. Let fame be the least of your goals as a day trader lest the need overshadow the commitment and the methodology.

Day Trading, Discipline, and Persistence

There can be no profit, no success, and no fame unless the trader has first mastered the self-discipline and persistence that are essential ingredients to profitable day trading. These skills are intrinsically intertwined in the psychology of the trader. My experience has taught me that the single most important aspect of any trading method, whether for the long-term, intermediate-term, short-term, or day trade, is the psychology of the trader. Without functional psychological tools, the best trading system in the world will be subject to the whims, fears, and hopes of the trader. The psychologically weak trader will undermine the system, and the result will be loss after loss.

My work with trader psychology dates back to 1968. The years have taught me well. I have learned that unless a trader has mastered his or her psychological ability to apply the rules of a system, no method or indicator will be effective. The lack of self-discipline will eventually take its toll in the form of losses. This will increase the trader's frustration, resulting in less discipline and more losses.

Systems cannot work and will not work unless traders allow them to work. The undisciplined trader will commit a multitude of errors, some conscious and others unconscious, that will undermine success. The errors will be those of omission as well as commission. Having been educated in clinical and behavioral psychology, I am well acquainted with the limitations of the trader and with the psychological roadblocks that traders constantly throw in their own paths.

In fact, I have written extensively on this subject. *The Investor's Quotient*, originally published in 1980, and *The Investor's Quotient–Second Edition*, published in 1993, have continued to be best-sellers over the years. Traders the world over have read both books. The many letters and calls I have received in response to the books have confirmed my assertion that without an effective psychological orientation to the markets, a trader is doomed to failure from the start. And this is especially true in day trading, where decisions must be made quickly.

Traders must be willing to realize their limitations, and they must learn and apply strategies to overcome them. While there are those who will disagree with me, I feel strongly that trader psychology is just as important as an effective trading system or method. Without both elements present in the correct measures, success will not come easily, if at all.

While many of you may choose either to ignore what I have said or to sidestep it entirely, I do sincerely believe that to do so would be the worst mistake you could make. Although it is impossible to completely discuss in one brief chapter what takes several books to explain thoroughly, I will do my best to acquaint you with the pitfalls that plague all futures traders, limiting their success.

Day Trading: Advantage or Disadvantage?

For many years day trading has been considered to be the most speculative of futures trading activities. I believe that this is a market myth that has been perpetuated by those who are unable to day trade or who are afraid to do so. The fact is that the day trader is in an advantageous position. The successful day trader understands the limitations of what can be achieved within the day time frame. The day trader is, therefore, the quintessential speculator. While the task that confronts the day trade is a formidable one, the rewards can be fabulous.

I see the day trader as a skilled surgeon, a sharpshooter, a race car driver. The day trader is focused on finding the correct target, taking aim, pulling the trigger, and bagging the prey. As mercenary as this may sound, that's what all futures trading is about. The profitable futures trader will keep his or her powder dry, taking aim only at the most promising targets. But the most promising targets for the day trader are not always those that have the greatest profit potential. The day trader must be careful to take aim at opportunities that have both profit potential as well as a high probability of success. This necessity serves as an advantage to the day trader. It requires the day trader to be highly selective about the markets that are traded, as well as the trades that are entered.

The day trader is also at an advantage in terms of time frame. Since a day trade is, by definition, a trade that is completed within the time frame of one day, the day trader is forced to exit by the end of the day either at a loss, at a profit, or at breakeven. This limits the profit potential, but it also limits the potential loss. Since one of the worst blunders a trader can commit is to ride a loss beyond its required exit point, being forced to exit at the end of a day will limit losses better than any other method I know.

Traders have an inherent predisposition to ride their losses and to take their profits quickly. Examine your own trading history if you doubt what I am saying. You will likely find, as I have, that your worst losses are those that were not taken when they should have been taken. As a day trader you will take your losses quickly. Hence, the day trader has a distinct advantage over the position trader, and it is an advantage that may be considerably more important than any of us is willing to admit.

Another advantage of day trading is that it allows the more efficient and effective use of margin. Since positions are closed out at the end of the day, there is no overnight margin requirement. Provided that the day trader is using a profitable system, margin will not be a problem. This means that starting capital can be somewhat less than what is required for position trading.

Finally, the day trader benefits from the fact that overnight price swings will not affect the day trader. We live in a time of immense market volatility. An open profit of $5000 in an S&P 500 position can turn into a $4000 loss overnight. A profit of $5000 on a day trade that is closed out at the end of the day is a real profit: one that cannot disappear by a sharply higher or lower opening the next day as a result of national or international events. This, to my way of thinking, is one of the greatest advantages for the day trader. Not only does it prevent the loss of an open profit, but it also makes for good sleeping conditions for those of us who enjoy resting quietly in bed at night *far niente.*

As You Read This Book

All futures traders must be consistent, efficient, adaptable, and persistent. These are the most important qualities that a futures trader can develop. However, because day trading is unique among the many different avenues that are open to traders, day trading has its special brand of psychology. Some of the systems, methods, and indicators I will discuss in this book have their unique caveats and considerations.

Please take notes carefully as you read this book. From time to time I will suggest specific methods that you may use to overcome your limitations and to maximize your strong points as a day trader. These are not necessarily listed in any one chapter or location in the book. They are scattered throughout.

The Importance of Self-Discipline

Chapter 15 discusses the psychological and behavioral issues that limit success in futures trading; however, before you begin to study the systems and methods I have developed, you will need a general overview of the qualities that facilitate or enhance profitable trading. The first among these is discipline.

Certainly by now you've heard the word *discipline* hundreds if not thousands of times. It is probably one of the most effete terms in all of futures trading. The problem is that merely saying the word is one thing; understanding its true definition operationally or on a behavioral level is a far more important thing.

What Do I Mean by Discipline?

Discipline is

- Not merely the ability to develop a trading plan and to stay with it, it is also the ability to know when your trading plan is not working and, therefore, knowing when to abandon it.
- The ability to give your futures trading positions sufficient time to work in your favor, or for that matter, sufficient time to work against you.
- The ability to trade again once you've taken a loss or a series of losses.
- The ability to ignore extraneous information and to avoid inputs that are not related to the system you are using.
- The ability to maintain reasonable position size and to avoid the emotion that leads to overtrading.
- The persistence required to maintain your trading system and to calculate the necessary timing indicators consistently, either manually or by computer.
- Above all, however, discipline is the ability to come back to the trading arena every day, regardless of whether you have won, lost, or broken even the day before.

You can see, therefore, that discipline consists of many different things. Discipline is not any one particular skill, but many. Perhaps the best way to understand trading discipline is to examine some of its component behaviors. Let's look at a couple of these.

Persistence. This is, perhaps, the single most important of all qualities that a trader can possess. Futures trading is an endeavor that requires the ability to continue trading even when results have not been good. Because of the nature of markets and trading systems, bad times are frequently followed by good times, and good times are frequently followed by bad.

Some of a trader's greatest successes will occur following a string of losses. This is why it is extremely important for traders to be persistent in applying their trading methods and to continue using them for a reasonable period of time. Those who quit too soon will not be in the markets when their systems begin to work; those who quit too late will run out of trading capital. Therefore, while persistence is important, it is also important to know when a trader has been too patient, remaining in the game when it is time to quit.

If persistence is so important, then how does the trader develop it? While the answer is simple, the implementation is not. Being persistent develops persistence. While this may sound like a circular answer, it is truly not. The only way to be persistent is to force yourself initially to do everything that must be done according to the dictates of your system or method.

Try this if you're having difficulty: Make a commitment to a trading system or method. Follow through with that approach for a specific amount of time, taking every trade according to the rules or, if the system is subjective, attempting to trade the system with as much consistency as possible. If you have been consistent in applying your rules, then you will find in most cases that your consistency will have paid off and you will have profits to show for your efforts.

Even if your trading was not successful, you will have learned a great deal. You will have learned that you can follow a system or method that you can trade in a disciplined fashion and, moreover, that the only way to do so is to be persistent by following as many of the trading rules as possible.

Compare this to the ignorance and confusion that come from haphazard trading or by applying trading rules inconsistently. Think back to your experiences as a trader. Remember your worst losing trades. You will find that those losses, which occur as a result of following a system or method, are easier to accept psychologically than those that are the result of breaking the rules.

Losses due to lack of discipline have often turned into terrible monsters, ultimately costing you much, much more than they should have, financially as well as psychologically. If you would like to master the skill of persistence, then you will need to practice it. Make the commitment, and you will see some wonderful results, even over the short term.

Willingness to Accept Losses.   Here is yet another important quality that the effective futures trader must either possess or develop. Perhaps the single greatest downfall of all traders is the inability to take a loss when it should be taken.

Losses have a nasty habit of becoming worse rather than better. Unless they are taken when they should be, the results will not be to your liking. Although it is easier on one hand for the futures trader to take a loss than it is for the position trader (since a loss must be accepted by the end of the trading day), it is still the downfall of many futures traders who are unwilling to accept the loss when it is a reasonable one. The disciplined futures trader must have the ability to take a loss when the time to take a loss is right. What's right is dictated by the particular trading system or risk management technique that is being used. I would venture to say from my experience and observations that perhaps 75 percent or more of all large losses are due to the fact that they were not taken when they were relatively small or when they should have been taken.

These are just a few of my random thoughts on the topic of day trading and discipline. Remember that in the day events, prices and trends move quickly. Decisions must be made almost instantly. Hence, your discipline and persistence are of paramount importance. There are many wrong things you can do and only a few right things. Know the right ones and act accordingly!

Summary

This chapter has acquainted you with some of the issues, assets, liabilities, and challenges that face the day trader. While there is no doubt whatsoever in my mind that day trading can be a highly profitable venture, I am just as certain that there are few traders who will consistently achieve success in day trading unless and until they understand the rules, follow the rules, master their self-discipline, and use effective trading systems and methods. The rest of this book will attempt to give you those tools clearly, concisely, and logically.

Remember that day trading is a dynamic process. Markets change, traders change, and underlying conditions change. Hence, as a day trader you must not allow yourself or your market understandings to stagnate. You must constantly be on the search for new methods, new market relationships, new techniques, and new procedures that will help you take advantage of current conditions. Where there are basic indicators and understandings that are perennially effective, there are always new perspectives and new methods. These can only be discovered by ongoing research and by ongoing evaluation of your current systems and methods.

2

A Review of Market Timing Indicators

I slept and dreamed that life was beauty;
I woke and found that life was duty.
ELLEN STURGIS HOOPER

As we all know, the quintessential issue in futures trading is *timing*. No matter how valuable a forecast may be, timing is the critical variable. There is a distinct and vast difference between a market forecast and market timing, and there is a distinct difference between a "feeling" or a "hunch" and actual market timing. Timing is quasi-scientific. A hunch and a feeling are emotional. Although they may be based on some internal sense of logic, they are not sufficiently operational or mechanical for use by the day trader. Hence, they must be discarded. They have no place in the repertoire of the day trader. Eliminate them from your bag of tricks. They will not serve you well.

This chapter is dedicated exclusively to a review of the major timing indicators that are popular among day traders. E.L. Thorndike, the "father" of American learning psychology, stated that there are millions of things a person can do wrong but only a handful of things that are right. Hopefully, this chapter will help you weed out some of the wrong or ineffective things while direct-ing you to those that can make you money as a day trader.

My brief review includes an example of each indicator, as well as my evaluation of its pros and cons. I will *not* discuss the meth-ods of calculating these indicators. This information is available in virtually any good book on technical market analysis. Although I may ruffle some feathers by making negative comments about your favorite indicators, I can only be objective within the scope of my experience and research as a day trader.

Traditional Moving Average Indicators (MA)

Whether you use one, two, or three moving averages, the concept is generally the same. Either the market price must close above or below its MA to signal a buy or a sell, or the MAs themselves must change their relationship to one another in order to signal a trade. A sample chart showing three MAs and buy/sell signals on an intraday chart is shown in Figure 2-1.

The Good News.   Traditional MA indicators tend to do extreme-ly well in major trends both on an intraday and longer-term basis. They will make you a lot of money when a major trend begins.

The Bad News.   Traditional MA indicators give many false (i.e., losing) signals. They will often get you into a move well after it has started, and when a change in trend occurs, they will often get you out after you have given back a considerable amount of your profit.

Hence, such moving averages tend to be very inaccurate and often have considerable drawdown as well as many consecutive losing trades. Figure 2-1 shows the buy (B) and sell (S) signals gen-erated by this method on a 5-minute S&P 500 chart. As you can see, the performance of the signals is marginal. There are numer-ous trades within the time frame of a day, all costly in terms of commission and slippage. Only the last trade of the day appears to be profitable. This is typical of MA intraday systems. They tend to trade too often, and they create too much "heat" (losses) and often very little "light" (profits).

Solutions.   Some of the problems with moving averages can be decreased as follows:

Figure 2-1. Triple MA timing (4, 9, 18 period) on an intraday chart. Buy (B) and sell (S) signals marked accordingly.

- Use a weighted, exponential, smoothed, or displaced MA.
- Use a different MA length to exit a trade than you use to enter a trade.
- Use different MA lengths for stop losses.
- Use another indicator to confirm or negate MA signals.

Variations on the Theme of Moving Averages

There are many variations on the theme of moving averages. These include MA-based oscillators such as the MACD (moving average convergence/divergence), the MAC (moving average channel), and various high/low MA combinations. A thorough discussion of the MAC method can be found in *The Compleat Day Trader*. (The MACD was specifically designed for S&P trading by Gerald Appel, while the MAC is my brainchild.)

The Good News. These variations on the MA tend to be more accurate and more sensitive than simple MA combinations of the closing price. The MAC can also be used to determine concise support and resistance levels. This approach can be very helpful to the day trader who wishes to trade very actively in the direction of the trend.

The Bad News. There is a tendency, as with many MA-based systems, to give back too much profit once a change in trend has developed. This is true of all lagging indicators.

Solutions. Here are some suggestions as to how one might overcome the limitations of MA-based indicators:

- Use a shorter combination of MA lengths for exit. Hence, exit will be triggered before the MAs indicate a reversal in trend.
- Use another indicator to confirm the MA signals.
- Use another indicator that is not MA-based for exiting positions.
- Develop a trailing stop loss plan that will enhance exit while not significantly diminishing system accuracy

Stochastics (SI) and Relative Strength Indicator (RSI)

Dr. George Lane popularized the stochastic indicator (SI). RSI is essentially similar to the SI. The difference is that SI has two values, while RSI has only one. The second SI value is derived by computing a moving average of the first SI value. Both indicators are often used to indicate theoretically "overbought" or "oversold" conditions. They may both be used as timing indicators as well as indicators of so-called "overbought" and "oversold" conditions.

The Good News. Both the RSI and SI have considerable sex appeal. By this I mean they look good on a chart. They tend to identify tops and bottoms quite well.

They are also useful in timing, provided one uses the appropriate crossover areas for timing trades. See Figures 2-2 and 2-3 for examples of SI and RSI, respectively.

The Bad News. The concepts of *overbought* and *oversold* are not useful, and they can get you into trouble. Both indicators tend to

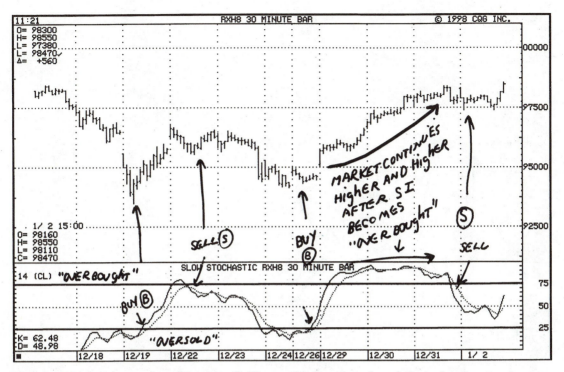

Figure 2-2. Stochastic buy (B) and sell (S) signals; how "overbought" stochastics can be misleading.

continue in what is called "overbought" territory or "oversold" territory for a long time. As prices move higher and higher, the indicator remains "overbought," and vice versa. The problem is that traders often equate the term *overbought* with a market top and *oversold* with a market bottom. *This is not always true.* Many times a market will push higher and higher while traders continue to fight the trend based on an overbought RSI or SI reading. The same will hold true in downtrends.

Solutions. Don't use the SI and RSI for determining overbought or oversold conditions. Use these indicators as timing methods when the readings cross above or below certain values. You might also consider using RSI and SI with other timing indicators.

Finally, I have developed my SI "POP" method that may be helpful in trading moves that occur in overbought and oversold territory (see my book *Short-Term Trading in Futures*). Another method of using the RSI and SI is to exit trades using a shorter indicator length than was used for entry.

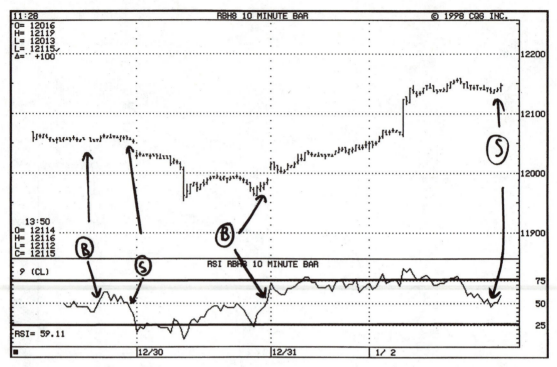

Figure 2-3. 9-period RSI on 10-minute T-bond futures showing buy (B) and sell (S) signals. Note that one method of using RSI is to buy on RSI values above 50 and to sell on RSI values below 50.

Chart Patterns and Formations

These methods are based on the traditional analyses as proposed by Edwards and McGee, as well as other methods such as those developed by W.D. Gann, George Bayer, and R.N. Elliott. There are many different chart formations and various outcomes possible for each. They require a good deal of study and are, at times, quite intricate. I have included only one example of these, since the literature is loaded with methods and systems based on these approaches. (See Fig. 2-4.)

The Good News.   These methods are highly visual. In other words, you can draw lines on a piece of paper and see what should be done. In addition, the methods don't necessarily require a computer, and they can be learned by almost anyone. Frequently

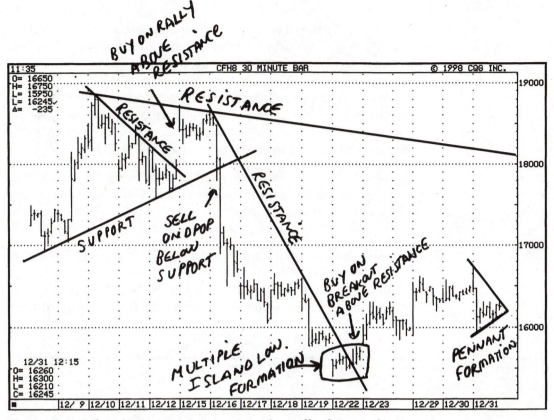

Figure 2-4. A few chart patterns on an intraday coffee futures chart.

the prescribed actions are specific, once you have completed the necessary interpretation of the chart patterns. The methods are usually quite logical. Hence, they have a good deal of face validity.

The Bad News.   In most cases, these methods are highly subjective and difficult to test for accuracy. The Gann and Elliott methods, for example, have been known and used by traders for many years; however, there is considerable disagreement, even among experts, as to what patterns exist at any given point in time and, in fact, how these patterns should be traded.

Solutions.   A possible solution would be to use the methods in conjunction with other timing that is more objective and operational.

Parabolic

The parabolic method is based on a mathematical formula derived from the parabolic curve. It provides the trader with two values each day: a sell number and a buy number. These serve as sell stops and buy stops.

Penetration of the buy number means to go long and close out the short, while penetration of the sell number means to close out longs and go short. I have included an example of a parabolic indicator plotted on a intraday price chart in Fig. 2-5.

The Good News.   The parabolic indicator is totally objective. It can be used as a mechanical trading system with risk management methods. In addition, it provides a buy and sell stop and is therefore capable of changing orientation from long to short very quickly.

The Bad News.   This method can get "whipsawed" badly in sideways or highly volatile markets (note Figure 2-5). The parabolic method can catch some very large moves; however, it has many of the same limitations that are inherent in the use of traditional moving averages.

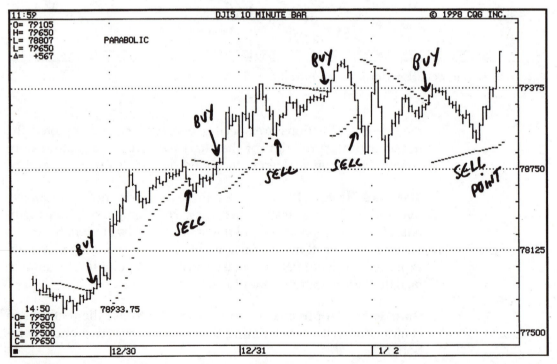

Figure 2-5. Dow Jones futures parabolic signals.

Solutions.   Use parabolic with other indicators that are not necessarily based on price, i.e., volume and/or open interest. Use shorter-term time frames for exiting parabolic trades. Also, since parabolic, in its pure form, is an "always in the market "system, you may be able to adapt it by specifying certain conditions in which it goes into a neutral stance (i.e., no position).

ADX and DMI

ADX and DMI are unique indicators based on reasonably solid theories about market movement. They are calculated with relative ease and may be used either objectively as part of a trading system or as trend and market strength indicators. (See Figures 2-6 and 2-7.)

The Good News.   These methods are not based on effete concepts or market myths. They are well worth investigating for development into trading systems.

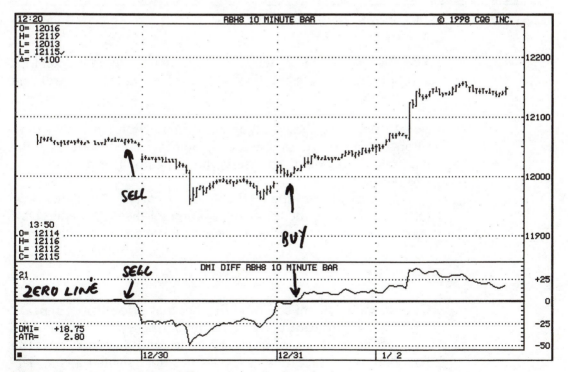

Figure 2-6. 21-period DMI difference on intraday silver.

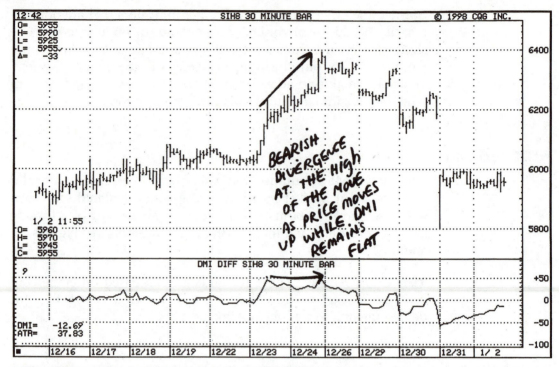

Figure 2-7. 9-period DMI bearish divergence on intraday silver.

The Bad News.   They tend to lag somewhat behind market tops and bottoms. As a result, they can give late signals that will cost you money.

Solutions.   Use these indicators in conjunction with other indicators that are based on different theoretical understandings of the markets. The DMI difference is the indicator I recommend for DMI work.

Use a derivative of the DMI or ADX as part of your method. In other words, compute a moving average of the ADX or the DMI and use the moving average to develop more accurate timing.

Cycles

Cyclical methods are based on the fact that price history repeats. There is a significant body of academic theory and research to support the existence of economic cycles and market cycles. The Foundation for the Study of Cycles has documented a considerable body of evidence to support the cyclical approach to trading. In addition, Jay W. Forrester at MIT has developed a highly intricate and statistically valid method of evaluating long-term economic cycles.

The Good News.   Cycle trends and cyclical patterns are relatively easy to find and can be subjected to major mathematical testing and evaluation. Price cycles exist in virtually every market and in many different time frames.

The Bad News.   Cycles are not always accurate. At times, cycle lows and highs are skipped; other times, cycles can bottom late or early or top late or early. Hence, timing is an issue of major importance. There is also some doubt as to whether cycles even occur on a very short-term basis. Dyed-in-the-wool proponents of cycles would argue that cycles exist in all time frames, although there is still insufficient statistical evidence to support this contention.

This does not mean, however, that cycles are totally useless for day trading. It is possible to extract cyclical tendencies that, when used with timing, can prove effective in day trading. See Figures 2-8 and 2-9 for examples of intraday cycles.

Solutions.   Use timing indicators with cycles. Do not make the mistake of thinking that cycle lengths are written in stone. Remember that cycles can be skewed. Tops can come *very late* or *very early*, as can bottoms.

Seasonals

Seasonality also has a lengthy research history. It is based on the valid and fundamentally sound idea that prices repeat their patterns within the course of a year, based on a variety of causes such as weather, supply, demand, and consumption.

Seasonals appear in monthly, weekly, and daily data. Seasonal patterns can also be found in spreads and in ratios. But the good news for the day trader is that there are also seasonals on a daily basis. We know for a fact that certain markets have shown a high probability of closing in a given direction on certain dates of the year and at certain times of the year. Such date-specific seasonal tendencies have occurred with very high degrees of accuracy in the stock market and in stock index futures. There are several

Figure 2-8. Is there a 210-minute average cycle in Japanese yen futures?

schools of thought on how best to study the history of such seasonals.

The Good News.   Seasonals are often specific and capable of being tested historically as well as validated mathematically. Seasonals can be used with or without intraday timing. Seasonals can also be validated with respect to current factors to determine if they are likely to develop in the present year.

The Bad News.   Seasonals have gotten a bad reputation in the last 10 years because of slick and dishonest sales practices by various futures options firms. This should not dissuade you from using seasonals, provided they are based on sufficient data.

In addition, several firms publish seasonal data based on limited history. The historical results of such seasonals are also suspect, so be careful. For an example of daily seasonal tendencies, see Figure 2-10. It shows percentage of time up or down closings over the last 19 years in June Treasury bond futures. Note that the per-

Figure 2-9. Is there a 320-minute average cycle in crude oil futures?

centages that appear in the bottom row are calculated on a daily-close to daily-close basis. The line plots show the average seasonal trend for the time frame indicated.

Solutions.   Use daily seasonals with intraday timing indicators or with trend indicators as a filter. (This will not always work, however.) Also use seasonals that are based only on a lengthy history base. In some cases there is only a base of 15 years. Try to avoid seasonals with less than 15 years of history. If you use futures options with seasonals, then use at-the-money or close-to-the-money options. Generally speaking, however, I advise against the use of futures options for the purpose of day trading.

> **Remember that seasonals are not perfect—*they do take losses no matter how high their historical reliability may have been.***

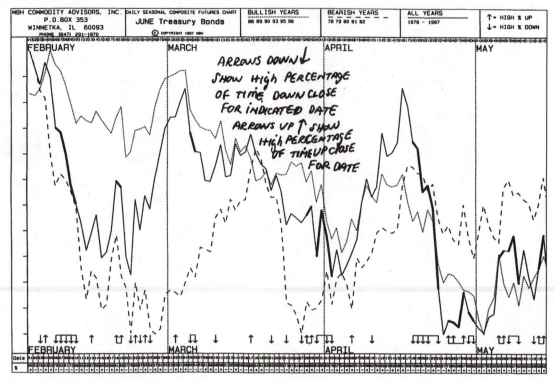

Figure 2-10. June T-bond futures chart showing daily seasonal tendencies.

Momentum (MOM)/Rate of Change (ROC)

These indicators are actually one and the same in the final analysis. Although they are derived using different mathematical operations, their output is the same in terms of highs, lows, and trends. I believe that both momentum and ROC have been ignored and underrated as trading indicators and as valid inputs for trading systems.

The Good News.   These indicators are very adaptable. They can be used not only as indicators, but they can also be developed into specific trading systems with risk management. They can also be used for the purpose of timing intraday spread entry and exit.

The Bad News.   They are lagging indicators to a given extent. As a result, they tend to be a little late at tops and bottoms.

Solutions.   Momentum and rate of change indicators can be plotted against their own moving averages in order to reduce the time lag of signals. Another way of improving the signals is to require that the oscillator remain above its zero line for at least two or three time units before taking action. The signals shown in Figures 2-11 through 2-14 have been filtered for this requirement. As you can see, it eliminates whipsaw-type signals. Figure 2-15 shows an intraday spread using momentum and its moving average to generate signals.

Market Sentiment Indicators

These indicators are based on the concept of contrary opinion. The idea here is that the majority will be wrong most of the time. There are several indicators or sources from which contrary opinion can be evaluated. These include *Market Vane,* the *USDA Commitment of Traders Report, odd lot short sales* (for the stock market), and my own *Daily Sentiment Index* (DSI). The theory is simple: When bull-

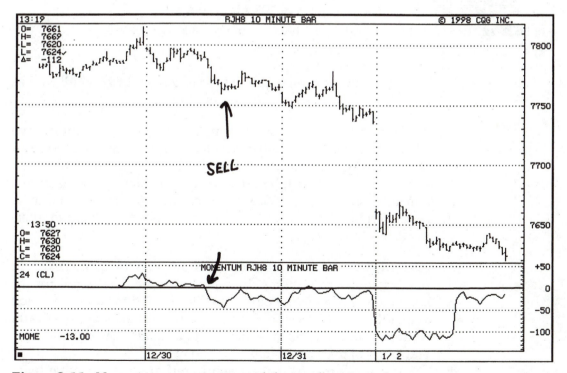

Figure 2-11. Momentum goes negative and the trend continues lower.

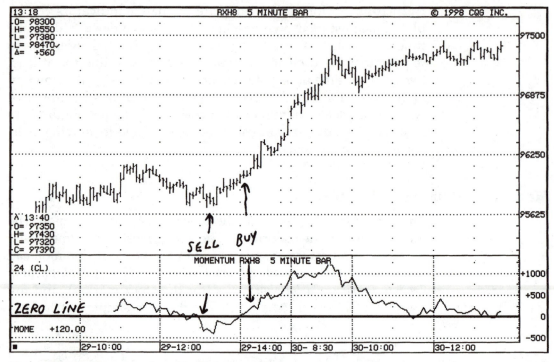

Figure 2-12. Price trend and bullish/bearish momentum signals.

ish sentiment is too high, prices tend to top, and when bullish sentiment is too low, markets tend to bottom.

The Good News.   Market sentiment and contrary opinion have a lengthy history of validity and reliability. They can be used in an objective way, preferably with timing and other technical tools.

In addition, they can be used with fundamentals and as inputs in neural network systems. Market sentiment indicators tend to be leading indicators. They can also be used for short-term and intermediate-term swings.

The Bad News.   These indicators are sometimes too early in picking tops and bottoms. In some cases the data is not timely, since there is a lag in the time it is collected and the time it is made available to traders. (To the best of my knowledge, my Daily Sentiment Index is the most timely. It is usually issued within several hours of market closings for the day.)

Some measures of market sentiment are not objective (e.g.,

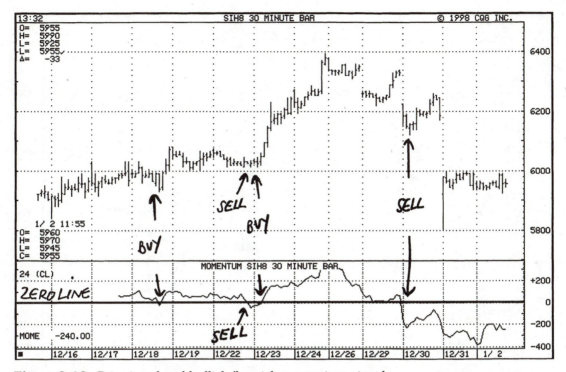

Figure 2-13. Price trend and bullish/bearish momentum signals.

examining newspaper headlines and stories for their bullish or bearish content).

Solutions.   Use these indicators in conjunction with market trends and timing. Use moving averages of market sentiment data to develop a timing approach.

Breakout Methods for Day Trading

Of all the trading techniques and tools available to day traders, those methods that use breakouts above resistance as buy signals and breakouts below support as sell signals appear to be the most viable for the average trader. As we already know from methods presented earlier in this chapter, this approach is often the most difficult for traders to follow, since it requires buying at a high price and (hopefully) taking profits at a higher price, or selling at a

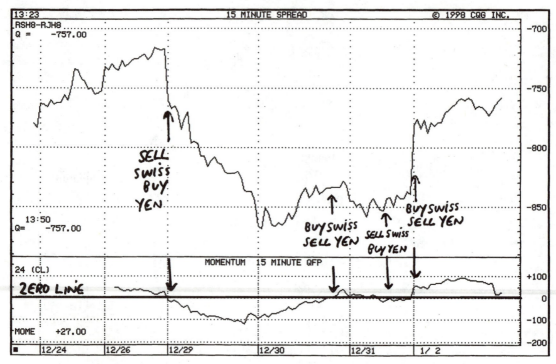

Figure 2-14. Swiss franc versus Japanese yen intraday spread momentum signals.

low price and (hopefully) taking profits at a lower price. Among the methods for achieving this end are several that I discussed in my first book on day trading, *The Compleat Day Trader.* Of these, the most widely followed is the critical time of day (CTOD). While CTOD was a good method and is still viable, I have developed another breakout method called the 30-minute breakout.

Another breakout method is my range breakout system. This approach is a day-trading variation on the theme of the Keltner-type resistance and support breakouts. Several breakout methods are discussed in this book. I believe that such methods are among the most reliable, most consistent, and most profitable for day traders.

Summary

This chapter provided an overview of the major timing and trend indicators most often used by contemporary traders. Of those discussed, only a precious few have merit for the day trader. I present-

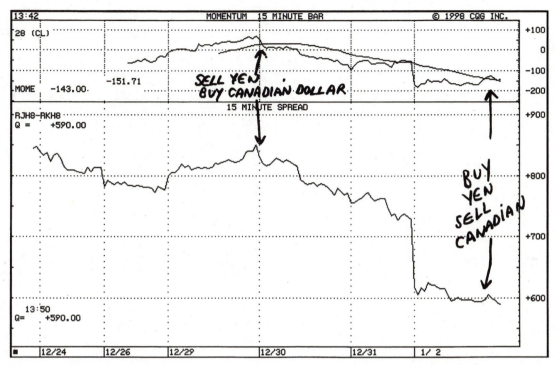

Figure 2-15. Japanese yen versus Canadian dollar spread with momentum and MA.

ed the pros and cons of each major approach, indicating how the limitations might be overcome. I rejected some methods as either too subjective or too inaccurate. While some methods and systems appear to make sense on a surface level, they do not make profits when tested or traded. Other methods were rejected as grossly inaccurate or as having drawdown periods that were too large.

The day trader has many methods, systems, and indicators from which to choose. This chapter has attempted to help narrow the field and direct your focus to the few approaches that appear to have merit. While there is a great temptation for the trader to be intuitive, it is always better in the long run for a trader to be objective, leaving as little as possible to the imagination. Objective, reasonably scientific, and mechanical systems are favored.

3

Day Trading

Art or Science?

Truth lies within a little and certain compass,
but error is immense.

HENRY ST. JOHN

Anyone who has traded the futures markets for a reasonable amount of time realizes fairly early in the game that method and technique go hand in hand; that art and science are inseparable. While much may be said in support of a purely mechanical approach to day trading, there is also a great deal of anecdotal evidence to support the fact that a good portion of success as a day trader depends upon the art of the science of day trading. I am not implying by this statement that anyone who is artistic in trading terms can succeed. I also believe that when closely examined, what may be considered artistic or intuitive is actually an internalized scientific approach.

Rather than accepting this possibility at face value, I'd like to explore, in some considerable detail, its ramifications for the day trader. While it may be unpalatable to the rigid day trader to accept the possibility that there is some art to the science of day trading, the fact remains that there is, to a certain degree. Let's explore the art of the science that will be analyzed and explained in this book.

An Issue of Discipline

The first and foremost area where art and science diverge is the issue of discipline. The simple fact is that discipline in trading is not inborn or easily acquired. Every trader has a penchant to subvert and pervert his or her market discipline. This occurs because of the involvement of ego and pride. Few traders are willing to admit to being wrong. Although it may be their timing methods that are wrong, they take the loss personally, and this ultimately prevents them from acting in a disciplined fashion.

Now enter hope and fear. These are the two emotions that ultimately transform a disciplined trader into an undisciplined trader; a good trader into a bad trader; a successful trader into a losing trader. And here is also where science becomes art.

If all traders were perfectly disciplined, then there would be no need for this commentary or analysis. But the simple and undeniable truth is that traders lose their discipline and revert to art, emotion, sensation, intuition, and random response. Were this not the case, the number of losers in all types of trading would not be as large as it is. Hence, we have no choice but to accept the fact that the trader can and will make mistakes based on his or her emotional, intuitive, and psychological responses to the markets. The real issue is what can be done to overcome the negative effects of such behaviors. Following are a few of my thoughts regarding the above issues.

Where Art and Science Diverge

First, let us be perfectly clear where art and science part company. Rules are rules. They are specific, operational, mechanical, and exact. Anything that diverges from these rules constitutes a change and/or violation of the trading system, method, or indicator. Therefore, it should be perfectly clear when a trader has violated the rules of his or her trading system. Note here that trading systems that are not perfectly clear in terms of their rules, are sitting ducks for rule violations that may go undetected. Hopefully, the methods and systems I have presented in this book are sufficiently clear, precise, and operational to allow a clear and concise determination of when rules are being violated. Therefore, any change in the rules constitutes a violation of the system and is clearly a step into art as opposed to science.

Art and science diverge when trading rules are changed, when trading boundaries are overstepped, and/or when specific procedures are altered. What were method and system now become art and intuition. The ability to discern and distinguish between art and science will be facilitated if your trading rules are specific and highly operational. Hence, I advise you to devise and follow precise and concise rules that are defined as clearly as possible. In both the long and short run this will be a great benefit to you. I do not discount the role of intuition; however, I assign it minimal importance.

When Science Has Been Transformed into Art

Clearly, the lack of specific and operational trading rules will precipitate the crossing over from methodology to mythology. In the long run this will not serve the trader well. It will prompt an emotional and intuitive trading style that will likely have losing results. There is, therefore, no choice but to do the following:

- Be aware of when your trading rules have been altered, violated, or circumvented.
- As soon as you are aware of the above, act accordingly to remedy the problems.
- Attempt to deal only with specifics when it comes to trading. Matters of opinion, expectation, and prediction are useless and counterproductive in a successful approach to day trading.
- Above all, maintain a fully disciplined approach to your day trading.
- No matter how intuitive you may be, remember that a methodological and operational approach to trading will ultimately prevail. Minimize your reliance on intuition.
- Refer to your trading rules frequently.
- Remember that even the slightest change in your methodology could have a major impact on your results.
- Know that just because a change in your system that has violated the rules has worked for you in the past, it is by *no means* an indication or a carte blanche that the same change in rules will work for you again.
- Refer to your trading rules as often as necessary in order to make certain that they are literally burned into your conscious and unconscious mind.

Art versus Science: What to Do?

Note that I have no complaint against art in trading. There are, in fact, many traders who are excellent artists and who are quite capable of using their intuitive powers in successfully trading the markets. They are capable of doing things that the vast majority of traders cannot do. They are talented, psychic, and gifted. As long as they are able to make money consistently with these skills, they are to be commended.

If, on the other hand, their skills are not capable of generating consistent profits, then they must question their methods, asking specifically if they are trading for profits or trading to make a case in favor of their intuitive abilities. Odds are that the vast majority of individuals who trade intuitively will be consistent losers. I am not denying here that clairvoyance exists. Nor am I denying that some individuals have an uncanny ability to predict the future (or futures). I am merely saying that for the overwhelming majority of us this method simply does not work.

The Best Place to Be

While I have the utmost of respect for those traders who have been able to achieve consistent success using their intuitive powers, it's clear that this does not apply to the vast majority of traders. Most of us are relegated to using our limited powers of intuition and psychic abilities. The best place to reside as a trader is in the home of discipline and operational methodologies. While I could likely write an entire book on intuition and psychic skills in the markets, this is not the subject of the present book. Nor is it my intention to imply that intuitive traders cannot make money. However, I will state clearly and without hesitation that if you want to succeed, you will follow the rules— whether these rules are mine, yours, or those of another writer or system developer. It's that simple, and it's that complicated. Follow the rules and, in the long run, you will come out ahead. Attempt to be psychic and, in the long run, you will lose money. If you are successful as an intuitive trader, then you are to be commended for being able to achieve what few traders have ever accomplished.

Day Trading: The Good, the Bad, and the Ugly

As a child I thought that life was blissful, that there was no evil in the world, and that somehow all of life's needs would be magically fulfilled. As an adolescent I was convinced that good triumphed over evil, that the more education I had the more money I would make, and that government exists to help us. As an adult I have come to realize that life is full of little disappointments, that things rarely turn out as we expect them to, and that the brutal, cold realities of life prevail.

But I have also realized that there is good news and bad news in almost every situation and every event. And futures trading is no different. Here are some of my thoughts on the good news and the bad news of futures trading. In reading my commentary, please remember the following: New traders are coming to the futures markets in droves; many of them lured to the trading arena by promises of sure profits from small investments. Take a little time and listen to the heating oil options ads on the radio and on television. Read the ads in trade publications offering guaranteed profits, and you'll see what I mean. (Before you put money into any course or trading program, make certain that they contain the proper risk disclosures.) Next time you get some futures advertising in the mail, read it carefully. Look at the claims and then reach your own conclusions about what the newcomer to trading is being told or promised.

Within this context, it's no wonder that so many people are disillusioned about what they actually experience when they become traders. But even veteran traders are not immune from the teachings of cold and hard experience with the futures markets. Here are a few of the brutal realities of futures trading as I see them. Take issue with them if you like, believe them if you find them familiar, or take your anger out on me for telling it the way it really is in the world of trading.

Most Trading Systems Just Don't Work

No matter how you look at things, the simple and painful fact is that the vast majority of trading systems work well in certain types of markets but not so well in other types of markets. The good news is that there are a *few* systems that have worked consistently over the years. The bad news is that their accuracy isn't very high. A system with 60 percent or more accuracy that has been a consistent performer for over 20 years is a rare find indeed.

What to do? You can abandon systems altogether and use timing methods and intuition. But this will work for you *only* if you have iron discipline and can take your losses when they're relatively small while riding your profits. Or, you can develop your own style.

Commissions Can Eat You Alive if Your Trading Method Is Marginally Successful

Paying reasonable commissions for your trading is important. To pay too much is to engage in a futile exercise. If you pay for service, then you must get service. If you do not need service, then do not pay for it. This is especially true for options trading. Some firms charge a percentage of option premiums as their commission.

Be very careful of these firms. If you buy an option that costs $2500 and the commission is 25 percent of the premium, then you pay $625 commission. This is outrageous! You could pay as little as $14 for that option at the right brokerage house. Even if you pay $75 for full service (which will get you a broker's input), you still come out way ahead.

Professionals Win, the Public Loses

It's that simple, that direct, and that predictable. It's like playing poker with a table full of professionals; the beginner will most likely provide grist for the mill. If you want to play the game with professionals, you will need to act, think, and trade like a professional. The bad news is that it's hard to do, but the good news is that it *can* be learned.

Do you Have Protection against Bad Price Fills?

The good news is that there are rules that will work for you on occasion. The bad news is that most of the time the rules don't work in favor of the public. Furthermore, the regulatory agencies that supervise futures trading will rarely be of assistance to you, since they are most often more concerned with making examples out of people with high visibility than they are in going after the insidious crooks.

Therefore, if you have a problem with an order fill, with a broker, or with an exchange, don't wait for help from the regulatory agencies; take matters into your own hands and complain directly to the firm's management or to the exchange itself. While it may be difficult for some traders to be forceful when they've been wronged, the fact is that the squeaky wheel gets the grease.

Misinformation and Disinformation Run Rampant

The computer age has made it even simpler for savvy operators to fool the public by creating seemingly perfect trading systems. The systems appear to be very good on paper but in reality are optimized to show the best-possible back-test scenario. In reality they have very little probability of going forward successfully in real time. Let the buyer beware. The good news is that systems are plentiful; the bad news is that most of them don't work.

Traders Love S&P Trading, but Most Traders Lose in S&P

Why? The reasons here are simple indeed. First, most traders don't want to hold S&P overnight because the margin is too high. Hence, they day trade S&P. What makes their S&P trading a losing proposition is the fact that traders use very small stop losses in this market. My work suggests that even a 500-point ($1250) stop loss in S&P is, at times, insufficient. When a market trades in an average range of 600 points daily, a 500-point stop loss is needed to take the daily range into consideration. The good news is that S&P futures offer great trading opportunities, particularly for day trading. The bad news is that a large stop is required and the odds of being stopped out, unless you use a wide stop, are very high.

Futures Options: Reality and Myth

As many of you may know, the good news with futures options is that your risk on a long position is limited to the cost of the option plus commission. Risk is, therefore, well defined and limited on long positions. However, although you will lose only a predetermined amount of money, the odds are that you *will* lose it. This is a variation on the theme of "if you buy you lose; if you sell you lose; but if you don't trade, you're missing a great opportunity."

At first blush, the idea of futures options seems reasonable and rational. After all, since most traders lose their money by staying with a position too long or by thinking too much, the idea of a fixed loss is very appealing. However, there are three important issues that many traders fail to consider and that many promoters of options fail to address: delta, premium, and time decay.

Premium is the dollar amount of the option. All too often, the premium on options is higher than it should be, based on the length of time the option has remaining and the value of the underlying market. Floor brokers mark up the premiums so that they can profit. In other words, they buy their options or create their options (by taking a short position) at wholesale prices, yet they sell them to the public at retail, making money on the difference.

Time decay is the perennial enemy of the options buyer but the eternal friend of the options seller. Since the vast majority of options expires worthless, it's the options seller that makes the money, while the options buyer watches his or her trade slowly lose value over time. Unless you are timely with your options entry and unless you pay a reasonably low premium for your option, your odds of success are relatively low.

A third and equally important options concept is *delta*. Very few traders have ever heard of delta and fewer yet understand its implications. Delta, in simple terms, is the degree with which an options contract fluctuates with its underlying futures contract. A delta of 90 percent (0.9) means that the option will go up or down about 90 percent of the amount that the futures market goes up or down. Options with low deltas tend to be options that have a very low probability of becoming profitable *unless* the market makes a relatively fast and large move in the desired direction.

An option for which you paid a high premium, that is close to expiration, and that has a low delta is, therefore, highly unlikely to be profitable other than in the most unexpected of circumstances. Yet such options are low in price and often attract the unsophisticated trader. Mind you, I am not saying that money cannot be made in options trading. I am merely stating that being a buyer of options is not where you will experience the greatest odds of success.

Insiders Still Reap
the Rewards

Although legislation and regulations have been enacted to keep the markets fair, the fact is that insiders are still the big winners in futures and options trading. By insiders I mean commercial traders and pit brokers. The good news is that futures trading still represents the last bastion of capitalism—the place where anyone with persistence, discipline, and some knowledge can make it big.

The bad news is that it's getting harder and harder to win as the markets become more competitive and as insiders grab onto opportunities before the general public has had a chance to do so. Fortunately, the basic rules of profitable futures trading still apply.

Therefore, if you follow the rules, you will improve your odds of success, even though they may be less than they would have been 15 years ago.

Your Odds of Success Are
Worse Now than Ever

I'm certain that this assertion will cause many of my readers—particularly those who are professionals in the futures industry—to bristle. But my opinions are based on good, solid, and lengthy experience. Can I prove what I'm saying by using hard statistics to back me up? No, I can't. But my experience counts for something, and it tells me, without a doubt, that there are fewer winners today, on a percentage basis (i.e., out of the universe of traders), than there were 15 or 20 years ago.

Believe me, I'd like it to be otherwise, but I just don't see it. The question is why. The answer is severalfold. First, there are many more green traders today than ever before. They've been attracted by the lure of advertisements for trading courses that pander. They've been promised that they can make a year's worth of income in the futures markets by starting with only a few thousand dollars. And they've been shown how they can generate several hundred percent of their money by buying heating oil call options for a seasonal play. None of the above is true. Still, they come to the markets like lemmings to the cliff.

Second, the markets today are more volatile than ever before. S&P futures trading is so volatile that a 500-point daily range ($1250) is commonplace. Given the fact that many traders have less than $5000 in their accounts and they want to trade S&P futures, the odds of their making money are slim to none.

Consider also the wide swings in virtually all other markets, and you have the necessary ingredients to small-trader ruin.

The third reason is based on an overabundance of information. While you may think that today's computer power and intensive research has helped create better traders, I disagree. The reality of this situation is that it has created an excess of information, which thoroughly confuses the novice trader and undermines discipline. The end result is that the average trader today is more confused and actually less educated than the new trader of 15 or 20 years ago. While good information is important, an excess of information will likely lead to confusion and obfuscation, as opposed to clarity and direction.

The fourth reason is that when traders finally *do* have profits in a trade, they are often scared out or stopped out of the trade(s) before the big move has taken place. Again, this is a function of volatility. While the nimble and experienced trader can use volatility to his or her advantage, the average trader and the new trader are only hurt by it.

Computers: Help or Hindrance?

In many cases and for many traders, the use of a computer for the purpose of generating trades won't help. In fact, it may hinder. Let's face it; most people aren't computer-literate. They have a very poor understanding of what a computer can and cannot do for them as a vehicle for generating trading profits. Only after a trader has defined his or her direction can a decision be made about the value of a computer in the trading program.

So if you're new to the futures markets and you can't afford several thousand dollars for a computer and software, then you need to put your efforts toward using simple systems that don't require the added expense. The fact is that there are many ways to trade without a computer.

Summary

This chapter reviewed the major issues and obstacles that await and confront the day trader. Specific answers were given as suggestions for overcoming the limitations and roadblocks to success.

I stressed that day trading, more than any other form of trading, should be considered as a science and not as an art. While the day trader has the advantage of not being concerned about overnight moves, the limitation of day trading is clearly that there is a limit to the profits one may make within the time frame of a single day. However, if the trader is careful to operate only in volatile markets, then the problem of limited profit potential will be overcome. Since day trading occurs within a strictly circumscribed time frame, there are rules and operational procedures that are unique to the day trader.

4

The 30-Minute
Breakout

Multum in parvo   ANONYMOUS

Of all the day-trading methods I have found or developed during my 30 years in the markets, there are few that can compare to the 30-minute breakout (30MBO) either in terms of simplicity or in terms of their ability to grab the "big ones." But do not forget that day trading is a two-way street: it can reward handsomely or sting painfully. While the 30MBO is simple to use, understand, and implement, it also requires the utmost in discipline as well as considerable courage, since it requires the trader to do the two things that are most difficult for traders to do. Specifically, 30MBO requires traders to buy or sell on a breakout to new high ground for the day or to new low ground for the day, and thereafter to maintain their position until the end of the day, unless stopped out.

Basic Method

The 30MBO rules are as follows:

- Do not enter any trades for the first 30 minutes of trading in the markets for which the 30MBO is being used (a list of suggested markets will be provided later).

- Make note of the high and low price for the first 30 minutes of trading.
- *After* the first 30 minutes, *buy* if the ending price of the 30 minutes is greater than the high of the first 30-minute price bar by a predetermined number of ticks.
- *After* the first 30 minutes, *sell short* if the ending price of the 30 minutes is less than the low of the first 30-minute price bar by a predetermined number of ticks.
- Your stop loss can be either a predetermined signal (i.e., fail-safe or "dead" stop) or the opposite signal (i.e., a sell signal after an initial buy signal, or vice versa).
- A trailing stop loss can be used to follow up an open position, since it has reached a given profit objective.
- In the event of a stop loss on a reversing signal, liquidate your current position and establish an opposite position (this will become clearer in the examples that follow).
- Exit your trade at the end of the day either several minutes before the close of trading or MOC (market on close).
- Trade only in active markets.
- If a long trade moves limit up in your favor, then take your profit; if a short trade moves limit down in your favor, then take your profit (assuming that the market you are trading has a daily trading limit).

The 30MBO buy signal is illustrated graphically as shown in Figure 4-1.

As you can see from Figure 4-1, a buy signal is generated when the market ends any half hour after the first half hour a given number ticks or more above its first half-hour high. The exact number of ticks is determined by market. The statistics for S&P futures are shown and discussed later in this chapter. Note that the signal can occur at the end of any half hour after the first half hour. Following a buy signal, the trade is followed up with either a stop loss or a trailing stop loss procedure (to be discussed). Now let's examine the ideal sell signal, shown in Figure 4-2.

As you can see from Figure 4-2, a sell signal is generated when the market ends any half hour after the first half hour a given number ticks or more below its first half-hour low. Note that the signal can occur at the end of any half hour after the first half hour. Following an entry signal, the trade is followed up either

Buy Signal

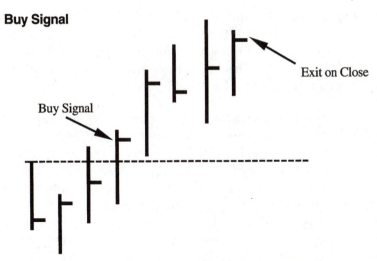

Figure 4-1. The 30-minute breakout system ideal buy signal.

Sell Signal

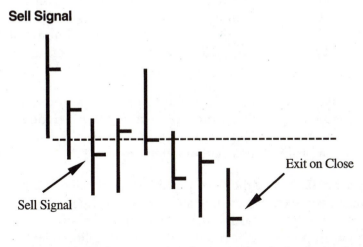

Figure 4-2. The 30-minute breakout system ideal sell signal.

with a stop loss or a trailing stop loss once a given profit objective has been hit.

Additional Parameters

Now that you have the basic rule, note the following additional details of this system:

Initial Stop Loss.   An initial stop loss is used. The stop loss must be large enough to give the market sufficient room to swing back and forth without stopping you out. In the case of S&P 500 futures, the stop loss must be large. Note the system test results presented later in this chapter for specifics.

Number of Ticks Penetration.   Typically, only several ticks "closing" penetration above or below the first half-hour trading range are necessary for valid signals to occur. The most recent results in S&P futures show that the ideal penetrations are 12 ticks on the buy side and 12 ticks on the sell side. These numbers will vary for different markets. However, as a rule, at least a two-tick penetration is needed. Note here that by a "closing" penetration, I'm not referring to an actual close of the market. It is, rather, the end of the 30-minute price bar.

It should also be noted that under different market conditions a different penetration amount could be used. As a rule, the more ticks closing penetration you require, the fewer trades you will have; however, the more accurate your results will likely be. The statistics for S&P presented in this chapter show the optimum values from January 1997 through late November 1997, covering 274 trades.

Floor Amount.   I have found it useful to use a "floor amount" for a trailing stop loss. In other words, once your 30MBO trade has reached a given profit objective, a trailing stop loss is used in order to lock in a profit in the event of a trend reversal.

Percentage Trail.   Once the floor profit has been reached, I recommend using a percentage trailing stop loss of the open profit. In other words, if the floor amount of $1000 open profit is triggered, then the initial stop loss is discarded in favor of a trailing stop that consists of a given percentage of the open profit equity peak. Assume, for example, that you enter S&P futures on a 30MBO buy signal. You place an initial stop loss of $2050 below your entry. The market moves up as expected and reaches the $1000 open profit floor level. You then cancel your stop loss and use a trailing stop that is equal to 50 percent of the open profit intraday equity high. The market continues in your favor and makes a new high for the day. Your new open profit is now $2000. At 50 percent trailing stop, a retracement of $1000 will cause you to exit the trade, going flat (i.e., no position). Assume you are not stopped out and the market continues higher, reaching a new profit peak of $3000. Your trailing stop is now 50 percent of the new open profit peak (i.e., $1500). If you are not stopped out and if there is no reversing signal, then you exit on the close using an MOC (market on close order).

Trades Per Day.   At times, a 30MBO buy will reverse to a 30MBO sell. Hopefully, you will have been stopped out at a profit before a reversing signal occurs. If, however, it does reverse at a loss, then you will take the new signal in the given direction. According to my latest work, you can take up to five trades within one day on reversing signals. Note that once you have been stopped out of a long position, your next trade must be a short position or no position at all (and vice versa).

Now that I have illustrated the 30MBO buy and sell signals in their ideal form, let's examine a few actual market examples, complete with their breakout prices, entries, and exits, to illustrate how the signals appear in actuality. Figures 4-3 through 4-10 show 30MBO buy and sell signals as captioned.

Stop Loss and Trailing Stop Loss

Since the backbone of many systems is the way in which they take their losses, it behooves us to spend a little time and effort explaining and illustrating the stop loss procedures. The 30MBO stop loss procedure is very simple but concise, as explained above. Use it!

What to Expect

The 30MBO is an excellent method for day trading, provided you adhere to the following rules and procedures. Frequently there is a considerable difference between what is described in theory and what transpires in reality regarding a trading system or method. Here are a few observations based on my actual experiences with the 30MBO. My observations are not necessarily presented in order of importance.

While the 30MBO rules of application are straightforward and simple to understand, many traders are either incapable or unwilling to follow the rules. This, of course, denigrates the validity and/or performance of the method, rendering it virtually useless.

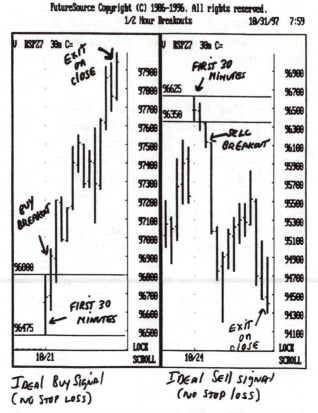

Figure 4-3. 30MBO ideal buy signal (left). 30MBO ideal sell signal (right).

The greatest difficulty in using the 30MBO is waiting until the end of the day to close out your position or using the stop losses indicated. Another serious difficulty is reversing your trade when and if the time comes to do so.

There is a great temptation to use a trailing stop once a profit has been made, or to add more positions. There are ways to do this effectively without jeopardizing your open profit. The temptation of most traders is to use a trailing stop loss that is very near the current market price. I have found this to be an ineffective approach. More often than not, you will get stopped out only to watch the trend continue in its existing direction. You are left with no position. My studies suggest that if a trailing stop loss is to be used, it must be a wide stop—in other words, a stop loss that is far away from the current market price. Typically, an effective stop loss

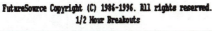

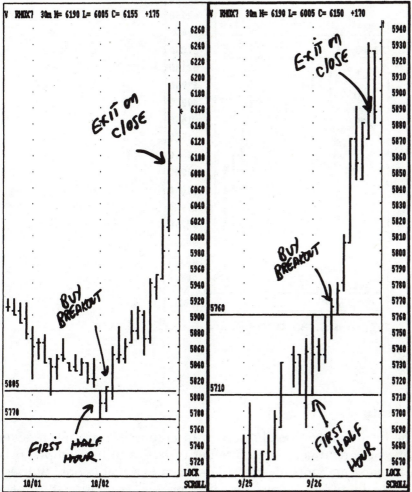

Figure 4-4. 30 MBO signals in heating oil on 10/2/97 and 9/26/97 (no stop loss).

should be at least 50 percent or more away from the current market price. In other words, you must be willing to give back 50 percent or more of your open profit on a given trade. I have included a statistical record of the 30MBO for two different time frames (Figures 4-11 and 4-13). Figure 4-12 shows the 30MBO in chart form. What do you conclude?

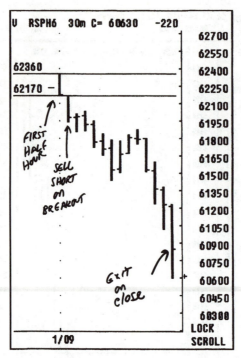

Figure 4-5. 30 MBO signals in S&P futures.

Analysis of Test Results

The historical test results shown in Figure 4-11 are impressive. Given the relatively large number of trades in my sample, it is reasonable to conclude that the system is a viable one. But test results, in and of themselves, may not tell the entire story of a trading system, good or bad. An accuracy rate of 65 percent might seem impressive, but this is just a surface impression that may not hold up under closer scrutiny. Closer examination shows that the results are consistent across buy and sell signals in terms of accuracy. Sell signals were 66 percent correct, while buy signals were 65 percent correct. The average trade after slippage and commission was $386.50, with long trades showing an average $312.50 profit per trade and short trades at $470.90 average profit per trade.

As in the case of all systems, the dollar amount of drawdown is

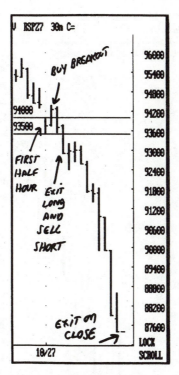

Figure 4-6. Buy signal and reverse to sell signal in S&P futures.

important. And in this case the drawdown of $9775 is very acceptable for S&P futures. The largest losing trade of $2125 is also reasonable for S&P. In addition, with a maximum string of only five losing trades, this speaks strongly in favor of the 30MBO system.

In testing systems, it is always a good idea to examine another time frame. Figure 4-13 shows another test of the 30MBO for the time frame from 1/11/96 through 11/27/96. This test covered 208 trades. Although the overall percentage of profitable trades was only 55 percent, long trades remains above 60 percent and the maximum successive losers remained at 5. Maximum drawdown was still reasonable, and the largest lowing trade was also reasonable for S&P at $2875. Even though accuracy was only 55 percent for this time frame, the average trade at $241.83 after slippage and commission was good.

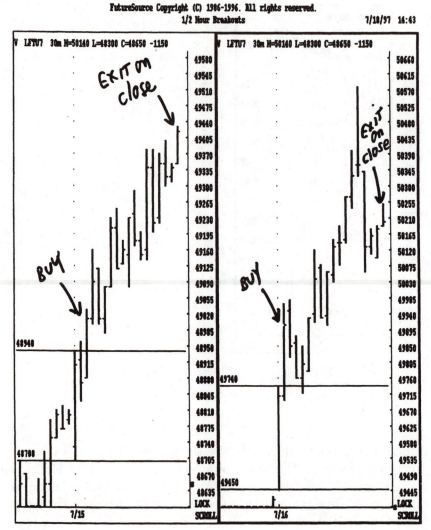

Figure 4-7. Two successive days of buy signals in London FTSE 100 futures.

Which Markets Are Best?

As with almost all systems, there are some markets in which the 30MBO performs better. Specifically, these are markets that have higher volatility and fairly large trading ranges. These are also markets that are more actively traded. For many years the markets

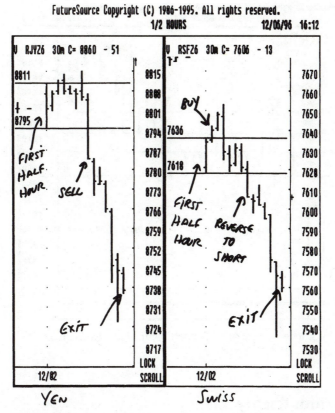

Figure 4-8. Buy signal in Swiss franc reversed to a
sell signal and sell signal in Japanese yen, both on
12/2/96.

most suitable for use of the 30MBO have been the major currencies, stock indices, Treasury bonds, the more active European markets (i.e., Italian Bond, Bund, DAX, FTSE 100, Notionnel), coffee,
heating oil, crude oil, soybeans, and wheat (when trading volume
is reasonably large).

In time, there will be new markets to trade with the 30MBO,
and some of the current markets may cease to be tradable because
of changes in trading activity. In some instances, special situations
may result in a previously inactive market becoming very active.
Should this be the case, the 30MBO will likely prove to be a viable
method in such situations.

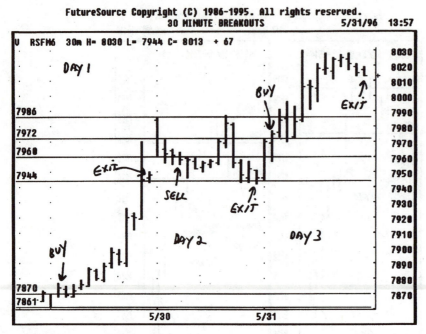

Figure 4-9. Three successive days of 30MBO signals in Swiss franc.

Risk and Reward: Reality and Rationality

No system, method, or indicator can be effective at all times. The 30MBO in its present state of refinement is not different than other methods in that it is not a panacea or the Holy Grail. It is merely a way of interpreting and dealing with the reality of the markets. And that reality is that systems take losses when they're wrong. The further reality is that systems can and will be wrong a successive number of trades on occasion. This reality is inescapable. However, it is not something that leaves us without an alternative. Here are some suggestions for dealing with the natural drawdown and inaccuracies of the 30MBO:

- When is the 30MBO best used? The reply here is similar to what applies to all trading systems. The best time to begin using the 30MBO is after it has experienced a series of losses. I recommend you find a market in which you wish to use the method and track its performance. After it has been wrong at least three

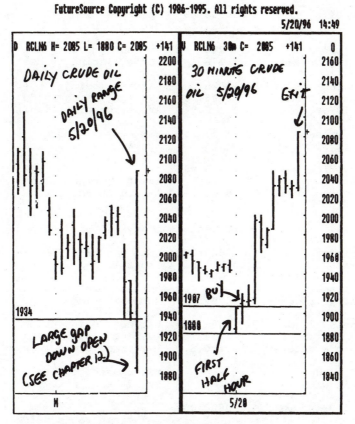

Figure 4-10. 30MBO signals tend to be more reliable on large-range and gap up or down days. Shown above is the very large-range day in crude oil on 5/20/96 (left) with a gap lower open, and the 30MBO buy signal (right) the same day.

times in succession, begin using the method. This will likely increase your odds of success, inasmuch as several losing trades tend to be followed by a fairly large winning trade.

- Be rigid with your stop loss procedure. Whether you have opted to use a dollar risk stop or to use the reversing method I have suggested, be consistent and rigid in applying your rules. Only by limiting your risk will the bottom line of your efforts with the 30MBO be successful.

- Attempt to trade the same markets consistently. Don't jump from one market to another. If, for example, you decide to trade jb.30min BreakOut #3 SP_E99.ASC-30 min   01/03/97 - 11/28/97

Performance Summary: All Trades

Total net profit	$ 105900.00	Open position P/L	$ 0.00
Gross profit	$ 246850.00	Gross loss	$-140950.00
Total # of trades	274	Percent profitable	65%
Number winning trades	178	Number losing trades	96
Largest winning trade	$ 10025.00	Largest losing trade	$ -2125.00
Average winning trade	$ 1386.80	Average losing trade	$ -1468.23
Ratio avg win/avg loss	0.94	Avg trade(win & loss)	$ 386.50
Max consec. winners	17	Max consec. losers	5
Avg # bars in winners	4	Avg # bars in losers	3
Max intraday drawdown	$ -9775.00		
Profit factor	1.75	Max # contracts held	1
Account size required	$ 9775.00	Return on account	1083%

─ ─

Performance Summary: Long Trades

Total net profit	$ 45625.00	Open position P/L	$ 0.00
Gross profit	$ 131525.00	Gross loss	$ -85900.00
Total # of trades	146	Percent profitable	64%
Number winning trades	93	Number losing trades	53
Largest winning trade	$ 6325.00	Largest losing trade	$ -2125.00
Average winning trade	$ 1414.25	Average losing trade	$ -1620.75
Ratio avg win/avg loss	0.87	Avg trade(win & loss)	$ 312.50
Max consec. winners	8	Max consec. losers	4
Avg # bars in winners	4	Avg # bars in losers	4
Max intraday drawdown	$ -9800.00		
Profit factor	1.53	Max # contracts held	1
Account size required	$ 9800.00	Return on account	466%

─ ─

Performance Summary: Short Trades

Total net profit	$ 60275.00	Open position P/L	$ 0.00
Gross profit	$ 115325.00	Gross loss	$ -55050.00
Total # of trades	128	Percent profitable	66%
Number winning trades	85	Number losing trades	43
Largest winning trade	$ 10025.00	Largest losing trade	$ -2125.00
Average winning trade	$ 1356.76	Average losing trade	$ -1280.23
Ratio avg win/avg loss	1.06	Avg trade(win & loss)	$ 470.90
Max consec. winners	9	Max consec. losers	4
Avg # bars in winners	4	Avg # bars in losers	3
Max intraday drawdown	$ -6625.00		
Profit factor	2.09	Max # contracts held	1
Account size required	$ 6625.00	Return on account	910%

Figure 4-11. 30MBO—back-test system results for 1/3/97 through 11/28/97. Parameters: Buy signal penetration 12 ticks. Sell signal penetration 12 ticks. Initial stop loss $2050. Floor amount $1100; 50 percent trailing stop. Five possible reverses daily. Exit at stop, reverse, or MOC.

Figure 4-12. Chart of market entry and exit points using the test parameters described in Figure 4-11.

```
jb.30min BreakOut #2  SP_E99.ASC-30 min   01/11/96 - 11/27/96
                    Performance Summary:  All Trades

Total net profit      $  50300.00  Open position P/L    $       0.00
Gross profit          $ 136825.00  Gross loss           $  -86525.00

Total # of trades          208     Percent profitable          55%
Number winning trades      114     Number losing trades         94

Largest winning trade $   5700.00  Largest losing trade $  -2875.00
Average winning trade $   1200.22  Average losing trade $   -920.48
Ratio avg win/avg loss      1.30    Avg trade(win & loss) $   241.83

Max consec. winners          9     Max consec. losers            5
Avg # bars in winners        6     Avg # bars in losers          5

Max intraday drawdown $ -10425.00
Profit factor               1.58   Max # contracts held          1
Account size required $  10425.00  Return on account          482%
```

- -

```
                    Performance Summary:  Long Trades

Total net profit      $  45475.00  Open position P/L    $       0.00
Gross profit          $  80700.00  Gross loss           $  -35225.00

Total # of trades          117     Percent profitable          61%
Number winning trades       71     Number losing trades         46

Largest winning trade $   5425.00  Largest losing trade $  -2875.00
Average winning trade $   1136.62  Average losing trade $   -765.76
Ratio avg win/avg loss      1.48    Avg trade(win & loss) $   388.68

Max consec. winners          8     Max consec. losers            4
Avg # bars in winners        7     Avg # bars in losers          5

Max intraday drawdown $  -4375.00
Profit factor               2.29   Max # contracts held          1
Account size required $   4375.00  Return on account         1039%
```

- -

```
                    Performance Summary:  Short Trades

Total net profit      $   4825.00  Open position P/L    $       0.00
Gross profit          $  56125.00  Gross loss           $  -51300.00

Total # of trades           91     Percent profitable          47%
Number winning trades       43     Number losing trades         48

Largest winning trade $   5700.00  Largest losing trade $  -2875.00
Average winning trade $   1305.23  Average losing trade $  -1068.75
Ratio avg win/avg loss      1.22    Avg trade(win & loss) $    53.02

Max consec. winners          7     Max consec. losers            5
Avg # bars in winners        6     Avg # bars in losers          5

Max intraday drawdown $ -13775.00
Profit factor               1.09   Max # contracts held          1
Account size required $  13775.00  Return on account          35%
```

Figure 4-13. 30MBO historical test on S&P futures for 1/11/96 through 11/27/96.

the Swiss franc, T-bonds, and crude oil, then do so consistently, attempting to take signals every day. Should you be unable to trade every day, then attempt to trade on the same day or days of the week in the event that there may be a day-of-week pattern biasing the results.

■ Don't trade markets in which the risk is too high. In other words, if trading in S&P 500 futures entails more risk than your capital and/or temperament will allow, then simply avoid this market. The good thing about using my 30MBO method is that it allows you to pick the markets you want to trade and to avoid the markets that are too risky for you.

Summary

This chapter presented the 30-minute breakout system (30MBO). I discussed the specifics of the method as well as the rules of application, limitations, assets, liabilities, uses, and abuses of this approach. I also gave you specifics as to which markets are best traded using the 30MBO. It should be noted that the 30MBO is not a static method in terms of indicator lengths. It is a method that must be adapted to existing market conditions. The adaptive and astute day trader will be able to readily discern when changes in market conditions require adjustments in the 30MBO. The 30MBO works best in active markets.

5

Day of the Week Patterns

It is not only fine feathers that make fine birds.   AESOP

Traders have long suspected that there are certain days of the week that are more apt to be bullish or bearish. Such myths as "turnaround Tuesday" or "trouble Thursday" have circulated among traders for many years. Some traders believe that if a market closes near its high on Friday, then it will likely move higher on Monday, or vice versa if it closes near its low on Friday. But there have been few definitive studies to either support or negate these market myths. Among the valid studies are those that have been conducted by Yale Hirsch in his excellent book *Don't Sell Stocks on Monday* (Facts on File, 1986) and Art Merrill in his classic book *The Behavior of Prices on Wall Street* (Analysis Press, 1984). I consider these two books to be among the best ever written on day-of-week or date patterns. Oddly enough, as outstanding as these books are, they seem to have been ignored by many traders. If you don't believe me, then try buying them!

We know that markets also tend to exhibit certain reliable behaviors on given dates that are not necessarily major holidays. The thinking trader will always be asking why certain patterns repeat. While I am certain that there are good answers to this question, I believe that it is beyond the area that is studied by a market technician. Hence, I spend little timing thinking "why thoughts."

Examples of Key Date
Seasonals

In order to demonstrate the validity of key date seasonals to you more clearly, I have included herein several examples. Let's first consider the daily seasonal tendency of T-bond futures prices from the start of futures trading in this market (Figure 5-1).

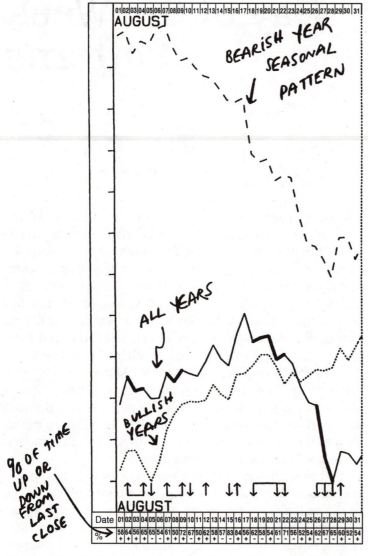

Figure 5-1. Daily seasonal tendencies in December T-bonds.

As shown in the illustration, there are three line plots on the chart. The most important of the three plots is the solid line. It shows the average direction of December T-bond futures on a day-by-day basis. Note the bottom row. This row shows the percentage of time that the market has closed higher or lower on the day. You will note that although the percentages are not particularly high on all days, some days stand out as significantly high-probability days for higher or lower closing prices (compared to the previous day).

August 9, for example, shows a reading of +72 percent, while August 22 shows a reading of −71 percent. (I have not preselected my sample in order to show the best probabilities. I have merely selected an active market that is traded by many traders.) The arrows up and down denote the highest probability moves of the month and their probable direction. While I am not saying that these patterns will always be valid, I do believe that there is something happening here—something that deserves the attention of all short-term and day traders.

As another example, consider Figure 5-2, the daily seasonal composite chart of S&P futures. Without a doubt, this is one of the most active and most volatile markets. The daily seasonal tendency chart shows the month of October for December S&P futures.

Note the numerous up and down arrows. There have been many days in the history of S&P futures that have shown a high-percentage reading for up or down closes (compared to the previous day). In examining the chart you will find a number of days with particularly high-percentage readings. I must point out that these statistics are somewhat questionable, since they are based on history dating back to 1982. Examining a longer history for this pattern would derive a more valid result.

Figure 5-3 shows the daily seasonal tendency for July soybean futures during the month of June. While the soybean market is not a market currently recommended for day trading, I chose it for inclusion, since the data history here dates back to the 1960s. As you can see from the chart, there are a number of high-percentage moves, as well as two pronounced seasonal tendencies during the month (denoted by heavy black lines on the "all years" line plot).

Further studies on key date seasonals can be performed by examining the data in a variety of different ways. We could compare the opening and closing price each day in given markets in order to determine if there has been a tendency for the close to be

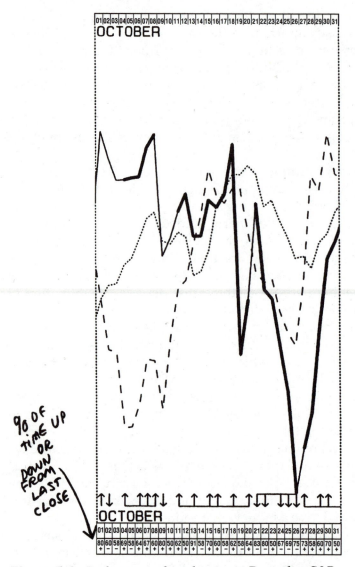

Figure 5-2. Daily seasonal tendencies in December S&P.

less than or greater than the open on certain calendar dates. When we perform such an examination of the data, this is exactly what we find. Again, the main consideration here is not whether we can isolate such tendencies, but rather, whether these tendencies are merely artifacts of the data (i.e., random events) or underlying characteristics of the markets themselves. I'm inclined to think

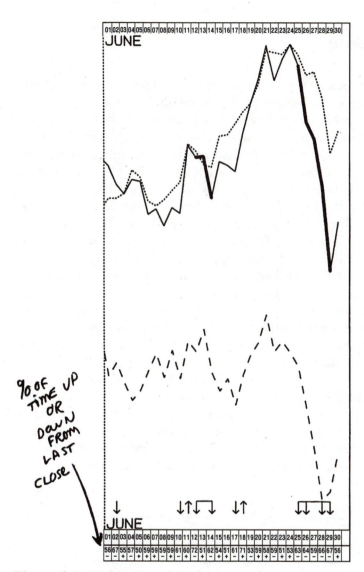

Figure 5-3. Daily seasonal tendencies in July soybeans.

that they do indeed represent patterns that are innate to each market; however, more research is required.

One way of improving the probability of key date patterns is to combine them with timing. In so doing we can hopefully capture the best of both worlds, allowing a timing indicator to validate or negate a pattern. This is discussed in greater detail later in this chapter.

Using Day-of-Week and Specific Date Price Patterns for Day Trading

Let's take a look at some day-of-week and specific date price patterns with an emphasis on their applicability to day trading. We'll begin with preholiday behavior. The premier researcher on specific date patterns in price behavior was Art Merrill. His claim that the price of the Dow Jones Industrial Average tends to close higher on the day before certain major holidays was supported with historical data back to the late 1800s. Merrill found an astonishing tendency for the Dow Jones Industrial Average to close the day higher than the previous day on the day before Christmas, Labor Day, Independence Day, Thanksgiving Day, and New Year's Day. His statistical analyses firmly supported his claim that preholiday behavior was not a random event. In other words, the probability of such patterns occurring by chance is about one in ten thousand!

Although the Merrill work was updated only through 1984, the pattern has remained valid. Consider the list shown in Figure 5-4.

How can the day trader take advantage of these statistics? There are two possibilities. First, a long position could be entered on the close of trading the day prior to the target day. The position would be closed out the next day. This, however, would not be a true day trade, since the position would need to be carried overnight. Another way would be to buy on the opening of the target day and exit on the close. While this would be a true day trade, it would not be a trade made exactly in accordance with the Merrill research;

Good Friday	60.9
Memorial Day	74.1
Independence Day	76.7
Labor Day	81.2
Thanksgiving Day	58.8
Christmas	72.4
New Year's Day	72.1
Total (all holidays)	68.1

Figure 5-4. Preholiday Behavior of the Dow Jones Industrial Average, showing percentage of time the market closed higher on the day preceding the holiday. (*After Merrill, 1984.*)

Year	Christmas		New Year's		Independence Day	
	A	B	A	B	A	B
1982	+	+	−	−	−	−
1983	+	−	+	+	+	−
1984	+	+	−	−	+	−
1985	−	−	−	−	−	−
1986	+	+	−	−	−	−
1987	−	−	−	−	+	+
1988	+	+	−	−	−	−
1989	+	+	+	+	+	+
1990	−	−	−	−	+	−
1991	+	+	+	+	+	+
1992	−	+	−	−	−	−
1993	−	−	−	−	−	−
1994	+	+	−	−	+	−
1995	+	+	+	−	+	+
1996	+	+	−	−	−	−
1997	−	−	−	+	+	+
	62.5% up	62.5% up	75% down	75% down	56% up	68% down

Figure 5-5. (A) Higher (+) or lower (−) close on the trading day before indicated holiday. (B) Close higher than open (+) or close lower than open (−) on day before indicated holiday, in S&P futures.

however, it would be fairly close in most cases. I have updated these findings for S&P 500 futures in tabular form (Figure 5-5) for the Christmas, New Year's, and Independence Day holidays from 1984 to 1997. What do you conclude?

I believe that there are other days that have shown a high probability of closing up or down. The task of finding such dates is not a difficult one provided you have the data as well as a computer to analyze it. My work has pinpointed many dates across all active markets that have shown a high probability of closing higher or lower than the opening price. In this case, these are pure day trades, since they would be entered on the open and exited on the close. A sample of such dates in several markets appears in Figure 5-6.

Market	Date	% of time	No. years in back test
S&P	1/5	72.73	11
S&P	1/14	81.82	11
S&P	2/2	72.73	11
S&P	4/12	81.82	11
S&P	4/16	80.00	10
S&P	5/19	80.00	10
S&P	6/1	80.00	10
S&P	7/14	81.82	11
S&P	8/27	72.73	11
S&P	11/24	87.5	8
S&P	12/13	75.00	12
Soybeans	1/5	71.43	21
Soybeans	3/18	66.67	21
Soybeans	5/14	68.18	22
Soybeans	7/3	72.22	18
Soybeans	8/21	72.73	22
Soybeans	11/7	70.00	20
T-bonds	2/17	75.00	12
T-bonds	3/29	69.00	13
T-bonds	6/3	85.71	14
T-bonds	7/2	78.57	14
T-bonds	11/23	72.73	11
Yen	1/8	73.33	11
Yen	2/2	75.00	16
Yen	3/19	71.43	14
Yen	5/6	80.00	15
Yen	6/21	86.67	15
Yen	8/27	78.57	14
Yen	11/21	75.00	16
Yen	12/23	68.75	16

Figure 5-6. High probability of close higher than open: dates in several markets.

Day of Week, Date, or Day in Month?

Some market analysts contend that date or day of week are not nearly as important as the position of the day during the month. For example, it might be more reliable to compare the opening versus closing price behavior on the first Monday of each month than to compare the opening versus closing price behavior on each April 7 in our data history. And this could very well prove to be a more valid approach. More research should be done in this area inasmuch as it is still one that has been minimally investigated and could, therefore, yield very profitable results.

The Monday Pattern

Yale Hirsch has amassed a vast amount of data to support his contention that Mondays are usually up days in the U.S. Dow Jones Industrial Average. Hence, his book *Don't Sell Stocks on Monday* admonishes traders not to be sellers on Mondays. My work supports this contention. My studies also show that since 1982, the start of futures trading in S&P, the closing price of S&P has been greater than (i.e., larger than) the opening price almost 50 percent of the time on Mondays (see Figure 5-7). One note of caution, however, is in order before I give you some suggestions for using the Monday tendency in S&P in futures 500.

> **There is no pattern, relationship, or indicator in the market that will always be correct. The best we can do is to approach a high degree of accuracy as a limit. All indicators and patterns will have their losing times. When this happens, the disciplined trader will take his or her loss and exit the trade. There is no other way to do things if you want to be successful in the long run.**

Now, getting back to the Monday pattern. One way to take advantage of this pattern in S&P 500 or Dow futures is to filter your system for buy signals only. In other words, assuming this pattern is correct, your best bet would be to follow buy signals only on Mondays, since the day has an upside bias. Consider this filter as an adjunct to the systems I have presented in this book and in my book *The Compleat Day Trader.*

Yet another way to take advantage of the Monday pattern is to buy on the close Friday and exit on the close Monday. This would not, of course, be a day trade strategy, since it requires holding the position overnight. However, it is very likely that buying on the opening on Mondays and exiting on the close on Mondays would have the same effect.

Are There Other Day-of-Week Patterns?

Based on my extensive work with a lengthy data history in all active U.S. futures markets, I find that there are indeed day-of-week patterns but not in the traditional sense. By "traditional sense" I mean in the "simplistic sense." Figure 5-7 shows the open/close relationships for selected markets based on day of week. This is a variation on the theme of the data presented in Figure 5-6, which shows open/close relationships on a calendar date basis. As you can see, the basic open versus close relationship in markets other than S&P futures is often little better (and at times worse) than a 50/50 event. However, with a small but significant change, the day of the week becomes important.

Day-of-Week Patterns with Timing

Yet another approach that I feel has great potential and applicability for the day trader is to use a day-of-week pattern with a timing technique. I have developed a specific method for doing so. I call

	Monday	Tuesday	Wednesday	Thursday	Friday
S&P 500	55.92	49.64	53.65	50.43	51.06
T-bonds	49.34	52.27	44.35	49.76	49.13
Swiss franc	49.69	48.16	49.83	48.42	50.60
British pound	52.56	50.50	54.26	50.81	51.24
Japanese yen	48.08	47.72	46.97	47.18	46.15
Crude oil	42.17	40.45	45.45	43.02	44.71
Soybeans	45.33	47.05	52.16	49.77	47.50

Figure 5-7. Day-of-week close greater than open relationships in selected markets.

```
jb.DBO System  S&P 500 INDEX 55/99–Daily   04/21/82 – 01/09/98

                    Performance Summary:  All Trades

Total net profit       $ 162500.00  Open position P/L    $        0.00
Gross profit           $ 429000.00  Gross loss           $-266500.00

Total # of trades           397     Percent profitable        77%
Number winning trades       307     Number losing trades       90

Largest winning trade  $   39425.00 Largest losing trade  $  -5725.00
Average winning trade  $    1397.39 Average losing trade  $  -2961.11
Ratio avg win/avg loss        0.47  Avg trade(win & loss) $   409.32

Max consec. winners          21     Max consec. losers          4
Avg # bars in winners         2     Avg # bars in losers        2

Max intraday drawdown  $  -27325.00
Profit factor                 1.61  Max # contracts held        1
Account size required  $   27325.00 Return on account        595%
```

Figure 5-8. The DBO method in S&P 500 futures—historical record. Long entry, three ticks, above Friday's high; short entry, 26 ticks, below Friday's low. Stop loss $3400. Exit on first profitable opening. (Reprinted with permission of Omega Research™.)

it dual breakout or DBO. The DBO is a method that buys or sells only on given days of the week based on a breakout above or below the previous daily high or low and on the open/close relationship of the previous day. This method shows a high degree of accuracy; however, it requires you to hold your position until the first profitable opening. In S&P 500 futures this means holding until the next day's opening. See Figure 5-8 for an example of the DBO history on Mondays (or the first trading day of the week).

DBO Rules and Parameters

The DBO rules are simple:

- Trade only on the indicated day or week (see historical records shown later in this chapter for day-of-week parameters).
- Buy on a stop x ticks above the previous daily high if previous close was greater than previous open.
- Sell short on a stop x ticks below the previous daily low if previous close was less than previous open.

```
┌─────────────────────────────────────────────────────────────────┐
│                                                                   │
│  jb.DBO System   S&P 500 INDEX 55/99–Daily   04/21/82 – 01/09/98  │
│                                                                   │
│                   Performance Summary:  All Trades                │
│                                                                   │
│  Total net profit      $ 143650.00  Open position P/L   $     0.00│
│  Gross profit          $ 398425.00  Gross loss        $–254775.00 │
│                                                                   │
│  Total # of trades            395   Percent profitable       78%  │
│  Number winning trades        310   Number losing trades      85  │
│                                                                   │
│  Largest winning trade $  11200.00  Largest losing trade $ –7900.00│
│  Average winning trade $   1285.24  Average losing trade $ –2997.35│
│  Ratio avg win/avg loss       0.43  Avg trade(win & loss) $  363.67│
│                                                                   │
│  Max consec. winners           18   Max consec. losers         5  │
│  Avg # bars in winners          2   Avg # bars in losers       2  │
│                                                                   │
│  Max intraday drawdown $ –23650.00                                │
│  Profit factor                1.56  Max # contracts held       1  │
│  Account size required $  23650.00  Return on account       607%  │
│                                                                   │
└─────────────────────────────────────────────────────────────────┘
```

Figure 5-9. DBO signals on Thursdays. Long entry six ticks above Wednesday's high; short entry 21 ticks below Wednesday's low. Stop loss $3500. Exit on first profitable opening. (Reprinted with permission of Omega Research™.)

- Exit on a predetermined risk management stop loss.
- Exit on the first profitable opening (FPO).

I stress that this method requires holding until the first profitable opening. Hence, it is not a day trade method, but it's as close to a day trade method as possible. As a point of information, it is often possible to exit these trades profitably in the Globex market after the official close of U.S. trading. Hence, this method can be considered slightly more than a day trade method and slightly less than an overnight method. Remember that, as a rule, I prefer *not* to trade on the Globex market, since liquidity is not acceptable at this time. This may change in the future.

Finally, please note that all of the historical tests in this book are subject to limits inherent in the Omega TradeStation™ software which was used in my tests. One such limitation is the ability to differentiate whether a market touched its daily low or daily high first. This could be very important in triggering a stop loss or in failing to do so. While the software is designed to test for such

```
jb.DBO System  S&P 500 INDEX 55/99–Daily   04/21/82 – 01/05/98

                     Performance Summary:  All Trades

Total net profit        $  –1700.00  Open position P/L   $       0.00
Gross profit            $ 311800.00  Gross loss          $–313500.00

Total # of trades            385     Percent profitable        68%
Number winning trades        260     Number losing trades      125

Largest winning trade   $   9375.00  Largest losing trade  $  –3925.00
Average winning trade   $   1199.23  Average losing trade  $  –2508.00
Ratio avg win/avg loss        0.48   Avg trade(win & loss) $     –4.42

Max consec. winners          13      Max consec. losers          5
Avg # bars in winners         2      Avg # bars in losers        2

Max intraday drawdown   $ –39100.00
Profit factor                 0.99   Max # contracts held        1
Account size required   $  39100.00  Return on account         –4%
```

Figure 5-10. The Wednesday DBO. Note that using the DBO method on Wednesdays (i.e., referenced to Tuesday's range) is a losing proposition in spite of its 68 percent accuracy from 1982–1998! This clearly shows that the day of the week is very important. (Reprinted with permission of Omega Research™.)

cases, it is not perfect. Hence, the results in these tests may contain some minor inaccuracies due to the limitations of the software.

DBO on an Intraday Basis

The DBO method can be adapted and applied to intraday trading. My research in this area is still in process, but the initial results are promising. Rather than use a day of the week as the reference point or bar, a given hour or half hour of the day could be used (i.e., similar to the 30MBO method).

Summary

Historical and statistical research confirm the existence of date and day-of-week patterns. Some of these patterns have shown a high probability of repetition over many years. By combining the day-of-week and/or date seasonals with timing and risk management rules, valid systems can be developed based on these patterns. At times, holding a trade overnight or until the first profitable opening will yield better results than holding only until the end of the day session. Keep in mind that risk management of these trades is just as important as it is for all methods and systems discussed in this book.

6

Trading Systems

Pros and Cons

Even God cannot change the past.

AGATHON

In my years of trading, I have met essentially four types of traders: the purely technical trader, the purely fundamental trader, the techno-fundamental trader, and the intuitive, seat-of-the pants, guts-and-glory trader.

The Purely Technical Trader

Although there are relatively few traders who are pure market technicians, there is much to be said in favor of such an approach. But being a pure technician should not be taken as synonymous with being a disciplined trader. Yet the technical approach, as long as it is not subject to interpretation, can be very helpful in the formula for successful trading.

The purely technical trader is more concerned with analysis and the realities of his or her technical indicators than in the news backdrop, the ramifications of politics on the markets, or the emotion of traders (unless these can all be quantified and expressed as indicators). While many traders fancy themselves to be pure technicians, they are, in fact, not as pure as they may imagine themselves to be.

They allow subtle external influences to creep into their decision-making process in spite of their supposedly technical bent.

The good news for market technicians is that they are apt to be more disciplined and less subject to the emotional reactions that are often associated with losses in trading. By remaining focused on their indicators, they will be less apt to respond to situations emotionally and, therefore, more likely to trade mechanical systems with strict discipline. Hence, the benefits of being a pure technician are as follows:

- Clearly defined rules for market entry and exit
- Specific rules for exiting losing trades
- Less likelihood of riding losses beyond their dictated exit points
- Greater likelihood of maximizing profits by not exiting too soon

Are there any cons to the use of a purely technical approach? Some traders would have us believe that being a purely technical trader ignores the realities of the marketplace. They claim that international and domestic events can, and do, have a major impact on price trends and patterns. Hence, they claim that the technical trader is like an ostrich with its head in the sand. The technical trader would retort by stating that a good technical system will anticipate major events, allowing the trader to enter before they occur or, at the worst, shortly after they begin. On the other hand, the retort to this claim is that some events, such as catastrophic weather or assassinations, cannot be predicted. The technician would reply that in such cases, which are few and far between, the system would protect the trader by taking a loss. Hence, risk management "saves" the system trader when the trading method is surprised by unexpected events.

The Purely Fundamental Trader

This type of trader is a rarer breed than the purely technical trader. Why is this so? The simple fact is that fundamentals are much more difficult to understand and to find than are technicals. Frequently, only a few insiders who are able to act on their knowledge well before the majority of traders have the news know the fundamental changes and conditions that precede or cause major market moves.

Furthermore, once a trader has the relevant fundamentals, they must be interpreted. Interpretation of fundamentals varies from one individual to the next. A given set of statistics might mean one thing to one trader but an entirely different thing to another trader. All too often the interpretation of fundamentals is a function of one's position. A fundamental trader with a long position will, therefore, be more apt to interpret a bearish report as bullish, while a fundamental trader with a short position will be more apt to interpret a bullish report as bearish. "Talking one's position," as this is called, is not unique to fundamental traders, but it is more common, since fundamentals are subject to considerably more interpretation than are technicals.

The benefits of being a purely fundamental trader are as follows:

- You will always have a reason or justification for your trade.
- Your trades will always make sense.
- If your analysis of the fundamentals is correct, then you'll catch the major moves.
- When the fundamentals change, you will be able to change your position.

Of course, all of the above are predicated on the availability of fundamental information and on its correct interpretation once it has become available.

The Techno-Fundamental Trader

This group of market participants is larger than either the pure technician or the pure fundamentalist groups. As its name indicates, those who follow this method either knowingly or by accident tend to combine technical timing and trend factors with fundamentals. Hence, when the fundamentals are bullish, the trader would be on the lookout for technical indicators that correlate with the fundamentals in order to fine-tune market entry. The justification for this approach (and it's a reasonable justification) is that markets do not always respond to fundamental changes immediately. At times there is a delay in the amount of time it takes for the fundamentals to sink in or to be assimilated by traders. Hence, timing in the form of technical signals will help the fundamental trader fine-tune entry. Theoretically, when both methods are in conjunction, the odds of success will be greater. The benefits of being a techno-fundamental trader are as follows:

- Timing will ideally complement fundamentals, causing them to work better.
- Timing and fundamentals together comprise the best of both methods in trading.
- Trades can be justified and understood on two different levels.
- Your trading will be responsive to world events, as well as to technical signals.

The Intuitive Seat-of-the-Pants, Guts-and-Glory Trader

No matter what term you apply to this type of trader, the fact is that they rarely follow any trading system, method, or indicator for more than a few days or weeks. One day they'll be singing the praises of triple moving averages, and then next day they'll extol the virtues of the Elliott Wave. Let their pet system of the day or week take a loss, and the love comes to a crashing end.

Such traders are rarely systematic in anything, tend not to follow a plan, tend to act on an emotional or gut level, and tend to be consistent losers in the markets. But why?

Summary

Trading systems are not the panacea to resolving the many limiting factors that are part and parcel of futures trading. The good news is that a trading system will give you strict rules to follow. The bad news is that most traders will not follow their rules. And finally, there can be more bad news if the system you are using has been overly optimized.

7

Power of the
Inside Day

I have stated repeatedly that my work with price patterns has revealed many interesting and potentially profitable relationships. Another important pattern is what has been called the *inside day* (ID). An ID is defined operationally as a day on which the low is greater than the low of the previous day and the high is lower than the high of the previous day. In other words, over a 2-day period, the second day's trading range falls within the range of the first day.

Traders have long conjectured that an ID is indicative of trader indecision and that a change in trend is likely to occur very soon. Logically this makes good sense. But good sense and logic in the markets do not always translate into profits. Let's take a look at a pattern that uses the ID concept to generate effective trading signals. Note in advance that this pattern deviates slightly from the pure day trade concept. I include it here because I feel it is an effective pattern, even though it requires holding a trade for slightly more than just the day time frame. In addition, I feel that the concept has potential if adapted to use on an intraday basis.

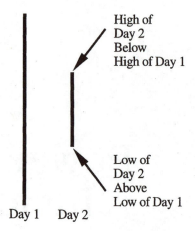

Figure 7-1. Ideal example of the inside day.

Inside Day Example

Figure 7-1 illustrates the inside day pattern. As you can see, it is a very simple pattern that is not only easy to visualize but also clearly defined in terms of a model or algorithm.

Figure 7-2 shows a daily chart of T-bond futures (day session only) with the inside days marked by arrows. As you can see, there are not as many inside days during the course of a 3-month time frame as one might expect. This is good because it means that signals generated from inside day patterns will not be too plentiful.

Inside Days and Trend Change

It may very well be true that an ID may signal a change in trend. But how can we take advantage of this relationship? One simple way is to use the high and low of the inside day as trend breakout points for buying on a stop or selling on a stop. The method is actually very simple. After an inside day, buy at the high price of the inside day plus x ticks, or sell at the low of the inside day minus x ticks.

The x ticks' value will need to be large enough to avoid whipsaw-type trades and small enough to give a sufficient number of trades. A risk management stop loss would need to be used, and some other rules would need to be associated with the method. If there is validity to the approach, then the technique should yield

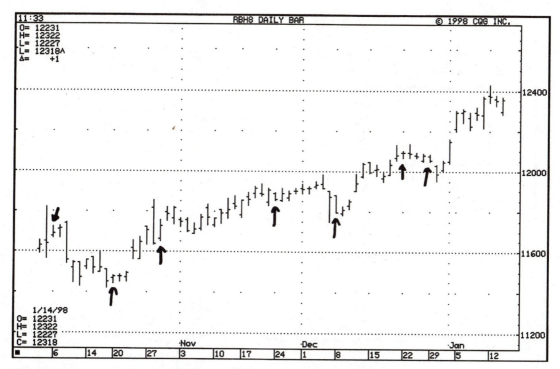

Figure 7-2. Arrows denote inside days (ID) in T-bond futures (day session only).

fairly good accuracy in valid markets. The ID breakout method model is shown in Figure 7-3.

Figure 7-4 shows the ID breakout method in practice. I have marked arrows at the buy/sell and exit points for S&P 500 futures.

Reviewing the Rules

Here is a review of the ID breakout method:

- An inside day ID is required before a signal can be triggered.
- *After* an ID, buy on a stop above the high of the ID plus *x* ticks.
- *After* an ID, go short on a stop below the low of the ID minus *x* ticks.
- The optimum number of ticks high for low penetration is a function of the market.
- Use a risk management stop loss.

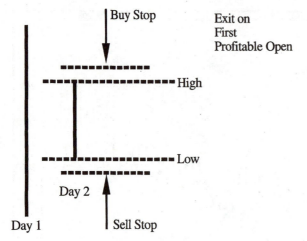

Figure 7-3. The ID breakout method model.

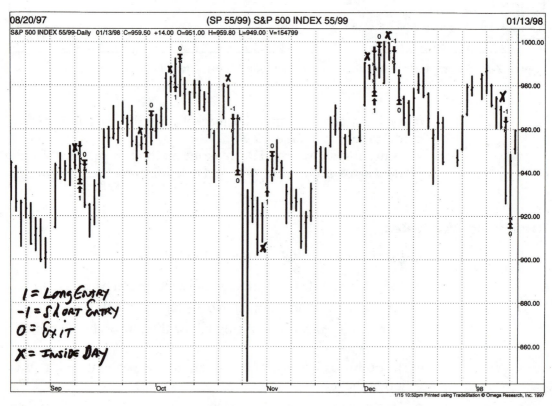

Figure 7-4. The ID breakout method.

```
jb.Inside Bar  S&P 500 INDEX 55/99-Daily   04/21/82 - 01/13/98
```

                    Performance Summary: All Trades

Total net profit	$ 94505.00	Open position P/L	$ 0.00
Gross profit	$ 379130.00	Gross loss	$-284625.00
Total # of trades	430	Percent profitable	69%
Number winning trades	298	Number losing trades	132
Largest winning trade	$ 20250.00	Largest losing trade	$ -5175.00
Average winning trade	$ 1272.25	Average losing trade	$ -2156.25
Ratio avg win/avg loss	0.59	Avg trade(win & loss)	$ 219.78
Max consec. winners	14	Max consec. losers	4
Avg # bars in winners	2	Avg # bars in losers	1
Max intraday drawdown	$ -21350.00		
Profit factor	1.33	Max # contracts held	1
Account size required	$ 21350.00	Return on account	443%

— — · · · ·

                    Performance Summary: Long Trades

Total net profit	$ 92055.00	Open position P/L	$ 0.00
Gross profit	$ 224730.00	Gross loss	$-132675.00
Total # of trades	246	Percent profitable	73%
Number winning trades	180	Number losing trades	66
Largest winning trade	$ 5875.00	Largest losing trade	$ -4075.00
Average winning trade	$ 1248.50	Average losing trade	$ -2010.23
Ratio avg win/avg loss	0.62	Avg trade(win & loss)	$ 374.21
Max consec. winners	14	Max consec. losers	4
Avg # bars in winners	2	Avg # bars in losers	1
Max intraday drawdown	$ -13725.00		
Profit factor	1.69	Max # contracts held	1
Account size required	$ 13725.00	Return on account	671%

— — · · · ·

                    Performance Summary: Short Trades

Total net profit	$ 2450.00	Open position P/L	$ 0.00
Gross profit	$ 154400.00	Gross loss	$-151950.00
Total # of trades	184	Percent profitable	64%
Number winning trades	118	Number losing trades	66
Largest winning trade	$ 20250.00	Largest losing trade	$ -5175.00
Average winning trade	$ 1308.47	Average losing trade	$ -2302.27
Ratio avg win/avg loss	0.57	Avg trade(win & loss)	$ 13.32
Max consec. winners	9	Max consec. losers	5
Avg # bars in winners	2	Avg # bars in losers	1
Max intraday drawdown	$ -31800.00		
Profit factor	1.02	Max # contracts held	1
Account size required	$ 31800.00	Return on account	8%

Figure 7-5. Historical record of ID in S&P futures—1982–1998.

- *Exit* on the *first* profitable opening or at the stop loss, whichever comes first.

With the above rules in mind, note the historical record in S&P futures from 1982 to 1998 in Figure 7-5.

Summary

An inside day can often indicate that a minor change in trend is imminent. The ID breakout method provides specific parameters for buying and selling on inside day breakouts. I presented specific rules of application for the ID breakout method. Note that this method is not a day trade approach. It requires the trader to hold a position until the first profitable opening after entry. Most often this is the very next opening. At times, however, if the trade is not stopped out, you may need to hold the position for a few days before it becomes profitable. The basic approach is highly valid and can be adapted to intraday bars within the trading day, at a stop loss, or at MOC. Note also the inherent limitations of this test as described on page 74.

8

System Testing and Optimization

Friend or Foe?

The verdict of the world is final.

ST. AUGUSTINE

The days of untested systems are gone forever. In fact, the pendulum is now swinging in the other direction. While unscrupulous operators once sold systems and methods for which they claimed fantastic results, today's unethical operators use statistics as a tool of deception. These individuals who, paradoxically, will benefit from the trend toward the statistical validation of systems can easily dupe the public. Manipulating statistics is not difficult. Just as Archimedes once said, "Give me a place to stand on and I can move the earth," the modern systems promoter would likely say, "Give me enough statistics and I can prove anything."

This sermonette on system validation makes the point that merely testing a system and generating highly favorable hypothetical results does not guarantee success with that system. Nor should such statistics be used as a security blanket or crutch by traders. Statistics can easily be manipulated, systems can be (and are) curve-fitted, and results, unless realistic, will not reflect actual performance when the system is implemented.

While many systems are developed to show optimum performance, it is imperative that systems be tested to show the worst-case performance.

Why Test Trading Systems?

Traders test systems for various reasons. Some test a system merely to say they've done so, only to disregard the outcome or to accept mediocre results, rationalizing the negative aspects of their system. Other traders test systems in order to sell them to the public—their goal is to optimize systems in order to show maximum performance. Then there's the serious futures trader who tests systems to achieve several goals, including but not limited to the following:

- To determine whether a theory or hypothetical construct is valid in historical testing
- To summarize the overall hypothetical performance of a system and to analyze its various aspects in order to isolate its strong and weak points
- To determine how different timing indicators interact with one another to produce an effective trading system
- To explore the interaction of risk and reward variables (i.e., stop loss, trailing stop loss, position size, etc.) that would have returned the best overall performance with the smallest drawdown

Test Your Trading System

While it may seem that the last item listed above refers to optimization, you will see from the discussion of optimization later in this chapter that it is not optimization according to my definition of the term. The purpose of testing systems is simply to find what will work best for you based on what appears to have worked best in the past. In so doing, we must remember that what worked in the past in hypothetical testing may not necessarily work in the future.

A thorough test of your trading system should include at least the following information:

Number of Years Analyzed.   Although it is desirable to test as much data as possible, many trading systems and indicators do not withstand the test of time. The further back you test, the less effective most systems will be. Many system developers test only 10 years of historical data, since that best shows their systems. You must make your own decision regarding the length of your test.

Number of Trades Analyzed.   More important than the number of years analyzed is the number of trades. You need not analyze many years of data if you have a large sample size of trades. I recommend at least 100 trades, provided your system will generate this number of trades in back-testing. If you are truly interested in determining the effectiveness of your system, the more trades you test, the better. Remember that there will always be a tendency to test fewer trades when you realize that the system is not holding up under back-testing. Some traders argue that the factors underlying futures market trends 25 years ago were distinctly different from those during the past 10 years. They feel that testing 25 years of data distorts the picture. If they were correct, how would we know when the current market forces change and that we must therefore change our trading systems? We are much better off finding systems that work in all types of markets.

Maximum Drawdown.   This is one of the most important aspects of a trading system. A very large drawdown is a negative factor, since it eliminates most traders from the game well before the system would have turned in its positive performance. Because most traders are not well capitalized, they cannot withstand a large drawdown. However, drawdown is a function of account size. Obviously, a $15,000 drawdown in a $100,000 account is not unusual; however, the same drawdown in a $35,000 account is serious. You may decide to risk large drawdown in order to achieve outstanding performance, but this is your decision.

Consider also the source of the drawdown by examining the largest losing trade. If the majority of the drawdown occurred on only one trade, you will be better off than if the drawdown was spread out over numerous successive losses.

Maximum Consecutive Losses.   This performance variable is more psychological than anything else is. An otherwise excellent trading system may have lost money on many trades in succession.

Few traders can maintain their discipline through four or more successive losing trades. Even after the third loss, many traders are ready to either abandon their system or to find ways of changing it. However, at times it is necessary to weather the storm of 10 or more successive losses. If you know ahead of time what the worst-case scenario has been, you will be prepared. That's why it's important for your system test to give you this information.

Largest Single Losing Trade.   This important piece of information indicates how much of the maximum drawdown is the result of a single losing trade. And this allows you to adjust the initial stop loss in retesting the system so as to see how large the average losing trade has been. If the average losing trade, for example, was $1055 and the largest single loser was $8466, you can readily see that a good portion of the average losing trade was a function of the largest loser. This shows that if you had a better way of managing the large loser (in hindsight, of course), your overall system performance would have been considerably better.

I strongly recommend close examination of the trade that resulted in the single largest loss if this loss is clearly much higher than the average losing trade. Another question to ask is "Why was the largest single losing trade so much larger than the stop loss selected?" A single largest losing trade that is several times larger than your selected stop loss points to a potential problem, perhaps with the system test. You must investigate further in such cases.

Largest Single Winning Trade.   Perhaps more important than the largest single losing trade is the largest single winning trade. If, for example, your hypothetical profits total $96,780, and $33,810 of this is attributed to only one trade, you have a distorted average trade figure. It's often a good idea to remove this one trade from the overall results and recompute them in order to show the performance without this extraordinary winner. You may find that the system you have tested is mediocre, perhaps even a loser, when the single largest trade has been eliminated from the performance summary. If you can wait 10 years for the one big trade, then use the system—but do so against my advice. What you're looking for in any system with regard to average winning and losing trades is consistency—far more important than one or two extremely large winning trades that give a distorted performance picture.

On occasion only several trades may account for a considerable portion of the net system profits. While some traders feel that this somehow diminishes the value of the system, I disagree. As long as at least one-half of the overall system performance is due to trades other than the largest single winning long and short trade combined, the system is valid. As far as numbers are concerned, I would not use any system that, after deducting reasonable slippage and commission as well as the largest single long and short winners, does not show at least $100 average profit per trade.

More importantly, because a large portion of profits in many systems derives from a very small number of trades, it is imperative that you follow each and every trade as closely to the rules as possible. Trading systems are not money machines; they don't grind out one profit after another. Trading systems make their money on the bottom line. There are many losers and few winners. The losers are kept in check by using money management stop losses that must, in most cases, be reasonably large.

And the winners, only a few of which are very large, make the game worth the candle. The trader who can't stick with a position, or let it ride, is the trader who will be sorely disappointed with the results, because the big winners will be cut short.

Later in this book I will make a case for systematic market entry and less rigid market exit. Bear in mind, however, that when this procedure is followed, you must stick with the original system as closely as possible for market entry. Such adaptations are recommended for the skilled trader only!

Percentage Winning Trades.   This statistic is not nearly as important as one might think. In actuality, few systems have more than 65 percent winning trades, and the more trades in your sample, the smaller this figure will be. Systems that are correct as little as 30 percent of the time can still be good systems, and systems that are accurate as much as 80 percent of the time can be bad systems. It's easy to see that even a high degree of accuracy with a large average losing trade and small average winning trade does not make a good system.

Average Trade.   This statistic will tell you what the average hypothetical trade has been. You must make certain that when you test your system, you deduct slippage and commission from your average trade. Commissions add up, even discount commissions. And slippage is an important factor when determining system performance. As a rule of thumb, I recommend deducting between $75 and $100 per trade for slippage and commission.

Once this has been done, you will often significantly reduce the average trade figure. As I pointed out earlier, you must also pay close attention to the largest winning trade and the largest losing trade when evaluating the average trade. The average trade figure is important, since it considers all profits, all losses, slippage, and commission.

Optimization

There has been considerable controversy about trading system optimization. What exactly is wrong with optimizing systems? Can you go too far? Is there a happy medium?

The real issues in system optimization are complex, and they've been exacerbated by the tendency of systems developers to optimize their programs above and beyond any reasonable degree. To optimize a system is to discover the parameters that provide the best results in hypothetical back-testing. In other words, optimization is a form of discovering what would have produced the best results using numerous if-then scenarios.

Before affordable computer hardware and software were available, optimization was a long and laborious procedure. To discover the best fit, the systems developer would need to repeatedly backtrack and test several variables. If the system parameters were numerous, the process was virtually impossible. Obviously, computers have made this a quick and efficient task. Now any trader with several thousand dollars can develop optimized systems.

Such ease of testing and optimizing is both good and bad. On the one hand, it allows traders to develop, test, and refine (i.e., optimize) systems much more rapidly. On the other hand, it has opened the door to what is called curve-fitting. The simple fact is that the powerful system-testing programs now available allow traders as well as systems vendors to repeatedly test a host of timing variables, stop losses, and other risk management schemes in order to determine which combinations would have produced the best results. In effect, this procedure fits the best parameters on past history to produce the best hypothetical results. However, the conclusions reached by such methods are often specious.

The trader who tests and retests to find the best fit will eventually reach his or her goal, but the goal itself may be nothing more than a reflection of the curve-fitted results. Tests tell us what has worked in the past but may not reveal anything worthwhile about the future. Since the past is not a carbon copy of the future, it is doubtful that the optimized parameters will work in the future. The more parameters in the decision-making model, the less likely they are to work in the future.

Overly optimized results lead to false conclusions. The result will likely mean losses. For those who develop and sell futures trading systems as a business, optimization is an amazing tool that allows the creation of outstanding hypothetical performance results that, in turn, allow systems developers to make incredible claims. And claims sell systems.

Time will tell if I am wrong about overly optimized systems. Vast personal experience, however, strongly validates my conclusions. I recall recent developments regarding several popular trading systems sold by a software developer. The advertised claims were fantastic. Systems were sold for T-bond futures, S&P futures, and currency futures. The outstanding performance claims provided a strong media campaign.

Naturally, all of the proper disclaimers were made to comply with the then-current regulatory requirements. There were no disclaimers regarding optimized results, however, nor was it disclosed that not all buyers of the systems would be using the same system parameters. Because the systems were continually optimized for best results, the hypothetical track records were truly impressive. However, the results did not jibe with results experienced by those who had old versions of the software—versions that did not reflect the new optimized parameters. This is high-tech deception. Recognizing that there might be legal liability, the systems developers eventually disclosed this fact in small print. Few buyers understood the meaning of the disclosure and even fewer cared, given the impressive hypothetical performance record. Naturally, buyers of the software felt that they could match the hypothetical performance.

In many cases, these traders did well initially. A customer in my brokerage firm purchased one of these programs and began trading it strictly according to the rules. The results were impressive. I began to watch intently every time a trade was made. It was uncanny how well the system entered and exited trades. It was as if the system had internalized a sixth sense about the market.

Then, after several months and excellent results, the system began to unravel. Numerous large losses occurred and performance deteriorated more rapidly than it had climbed. The dangers of an overly optimized system became apparent once again.

A Rational Approach to System Development

I do not totally oppose optimizing trading systems; however, I do favor a rational approach to this procedure. My rule of thumb is simple: Your trading system should have no more than four to six variables. You should search for the best combination of entry and exit variables, as well as a reasonable combination of stop loss and trailing stop loss amounts. But this is where the optimization should end. The more variables you build into the system, the less likely will be the future performance of the parameters.

Another aspect of system development relates to market personality—a topic that has received little attention by most traders and market analysts. Rather than heavily optimizing a system, I recommend tailoring your system to the personality characteristics of the individual markets, provided that such characteristics exist and that they are sufficiently stable.

Summary

The development and testing of trading systems is perhaps one of the three most important issues in trading. System results can be specious if the developer uses faulty rules, optimizes excessively, or fails to understand the differences between reality and fantasy. Armed with a computer, historical data, and a few ideas, a trader can easily fall into the trench of highly optimized systems that look good on paper but that fail to produce results commensurate with the back-test.

In addition, guidelines for effective system development were presented with the proper caveats. I defined a number of terms and gave you some ideas of how to differentiate systems that were likely to go forward with similar results to their back-tests and systems that were unlikely to perform as expected.

9
Emotions, Traders, and Markets

Madness is rare in individuals, but in groups,
parties, nations and ages, it is the rule...
FRIEDRICH NIETZSCHE

In his brief but powerful commentary on the nature of insanity and human emotion, Friedrich Nietzsche unknowingly but explicitly described the nature of the human condition in the stock and futures markets. To apply his profound words to the markets is, perhaps, to pervert his intent, yet they are so deeply apropos that the comparison begs to be made. For the day trader intent upon success, Nietzche's words may well prove to be a cornerstone of market fact.

The history of humankind is the history of speculation. In one form or another, speculation dates back thousands of years to the earliest days of recorded history. Our forebears speculated daily on the weather in their search for shelter. In growing crops and in warding off hostile animals and aggressors, their speculative ventures became matters of life and death. Whether for the purpose of survival or success in business, risk taking has always been a vital and necessary part of life on our planet.

With risk and speculation, however, come the inevitable and unavoidable consequences and evils of emotion. We fear that our decisions will lead to pain or losses, and we are therefore ready victims of other emotional and behavioral consequences. We fear that failure to take action will lead to negative consequences, so we act impulsively. Impulse is the primary enemy of all traders; however, it can be particularly destructive to the day trader.

We seek to protect what we have gained for fear it will be lost or that its quantity may be diminished. We are motivated by greed to expect large profits from small investments, which causes us to ignore our rational thoughts and prompts us to act on emotion. There are literally thousands of human behaviors that are motivated by the expectation of financial gain or by the fear of financial loss.

Even a cursory study of world financial history leads to the inescapable conclusion that there has always been a close relationship between the intensity of human emotions and significant market turning points. Whether novices or seasoned veterans, investors and traders know that the madness of crowds is often hard at work when markets establish major tops and bottoms. As a day trader, you will need to keep your emotions in check at all times, since the intensity of emotional expression is most readily observed within the trading day and in response to news reports, international events, and crises.

We know, almost intuitively, that the crowd will be wrong most of the time. In order to avoid being trampled to death in a burning theater, we must choose the exit that the mob has not chosen. To survive financial panics and crashes, it is imperative for us to muster every ounce of courage so that we may buy when the "whole world" is selling or sell when the panicked crowd is in a buying frenzy.

We know from repeated and often costly experience that those who can buy into crashes and panics will be successful, while those who can sell into buying panics will also profit handsomely. Yet we are also painfully cognizant of the fact that to do so runs totally contrary to the primordial maps that have shaped our behavior for hundreds and thousands of years. The "fight or flight" response causes us to fight markets or to flee from them, rather than to evaluate them objectively and unemotionally.

Emotional extremes correlate closely with major market tops and bottoms. This correlation can be readily ascertained by examining certain evidence such as newspaper accounts, magazine articles, television and radio reports (where available), and trader anecdotes. Study them to know whether a market is close to bottoming or topping. When the news is most bullish a top is imminent. Pervasive bearish news suggests a bottom. Many of the day-trading indicators discussed in this book translate emotion in market methodology.

Various technical market indicators such as trading volume, specific chart formations, and timing signals also have shown considerable predictive validity when correlated with measures of investor emotion, particularly in the day time frame. Mob psychology is clearly in evidence at virtually all major market tops and bottoms. Emotion can be your worst enemy or it can be your best friend. Make it your friend and ally in the day time frame, for it is a formidable enemy that cannot be defeated. In order to do this, you will need to rely on objective, operational, and definable methods.

Develop Your Rules

In order to steer your emotions in a positive direction, you must follow certain general rules. To those who have been in the markets for many years, the time-tested and oft-repeated trading rules are well known. In fact, they are so well known that few of us give them sufficient attention.

If you understand these important rules in the light of your personal psychology, you may be more willing to use them. I have found it very useful to keep a list of these rules where I can refer to them often; they help keep me on the right track.

- *Plan your day trades and keep them available for reference.* If you are specific, organized, and act on plans, you will avoid costly efforts often caused by spontaneous decisions. A concise day-trading plan will help you avoid the losses that can arise from acting impulsively. In short, plan your trades and trade your plans.
- *You alone are responsible for your success or failure.* You must assume total responsibility for results, good or bad. You alone are the vehicle to profits and losses. By assuming total responsibility and not blaming brokers, friends, or market letters for errors, you accept the seriousness of trading. You will learn that the situation is entirely under your own control. This will make you consistent and truthful to your trading system, which is the

single most valuable key to success as a position trader or as a day trader.

■ *Never hope that a day trade will go your way; never fear that a day trade will not go your way.* Both attitudes lead to unrealistic expectations, emotionally inspired decisions, and negative attitudes. A day trade, once established, will result in whatever market action prevails.

Once the trade has been made, its fate is sealed and no amount of hope or fear will make things different. Hope and fear are two of the greatest enemies of the day trader, fostering only false perceptions. You must avoid these feelings at all costs. If your system says to exit, then do so. Do not carry your day trade overnight *unless* your system so dictates.

■ *Monitor your performance—feedback is important.* One of the most important things a day trader can know about his or her system is whether it is working. The only way to know this is by keeping a thorough record of results. This will also provide the feedback necessary to reward you for good trading. At any time you must know how well or how poorly you are doing.

■ *A positive attitude is your greatest asset.* A good day-trading system is perhaps only 20 percent of the total picture. A positive attitude may very well compose the balance of successful trading. You must constantly be aware that the enemies of profitable investing and speculation are never absent. The only way to combat the negative effects of losses, interference from others, and poor trading signals is by the maintenance of a positive attitude, regardless of how bad things may seem. I know that this is more easily said than done.

■ *Cultivate effective and positive relationships.* We are known by the company we keep. Moreover, we are influenced by those around us. If we surround ourselves with losers, loafers, pretenders, depressives, or whiners, we will not learn any positive skills. If we associate with those who are highly motivated, who seek to achieve, who have ambitious goals, and who are willing to forge ahead regardless of obstacles, then we will acquire similar goals. Personal relationships, as well as business associations, should be cultivated along these general guidelines.

■ *Don't take the market home with you.* If you day trade for a living, then you must take great care to leave the market when you leave the office. Even if you are only a part-time trader and do not have a full-time market-related job, you must also avoid spending too much time or thought on the markets. When things go well, you may allow the markets to have too much influence in fulfilling other areas of your life. This is not advisable, since it will cause you to avoid or delay solving other problems.

Trading must be considered a means to an end. It should not become a way of life, and it should not dictate your every move. Make certain you take vacations. Take time each year to get away from it all. By being too close to the situation, you may not see it for what it really is.

■ *Enjoy the fruits of your labor—spend some profits, save some profits.* Make it a regular practice to remove profits from the market. Spend some of them and save some of them. You must directly experience the positive feelings of using profits to acquire some of the things you have always wanted to buy. I suggest you do this regularly, perhaps monthly. You will not be motivated to make profits if you do not experience firsthand the enjoyment that can come from spending money.

■ *Avoid overconfidence—it could be your greatest enemy.* Day trading does not always move in a positive direction. Just as you should not allow your losing day to bring you down, you must not allow the winning day to get you up too high. If you are on either of these emotional extremes, your judgment can be impaired and you will not be rational enough to trade effectively. You will be either too brave or too meek. The best course is to even out the peaks and valleys. Each loss should be a negative experience, but not a totally destructive defeat. Similarly, each profit should be taken in stride.

■ *Your next goal should always be in sight.* Once you have attained an objective, make certain that your next challenge is set. A well-known commodity trader made several million dollars in the market one year. He lost it and almost went bankrupt the next year. I asked him how this could have happened. "Simple," he replied. "When you climb a mountain and you are sitting on the top of the world, it gets lonely. There's no place left to go but down." If, however, you have another mountain to climb once you get to the top, you will not be tempted to go down in order to have a new challenge.

Systems Trading, Discipline, and Profits

> Cut your losses and let your profits ride. The big money is made in the big pull. Don't add to a losing position. Always use stop losses. Don't meet margin calls. When in doubt, stay out. The trend is your friend.

The clichés are worn and weary. By now you've heard the rules about trading discipline at least a thousand times, and you're tired of hearing them. To most traders these rules are nothing more than words—simple to understand but near impossible to implement. And there seems to be little anyone can do to drive the point home.

Traders are only human and, as a consequence, are subject to the frailties of the human ego. We are unwilling to accept losses, unhappy when profits are small, afraid when prices are too low, and too brave when prices are high. Regardless of how often traders take losses, they rarely learn from them. In one form or another, this subject has been the focal point of numerous books, tapes, seminars, courses, and psychoanalysts' couches. Sad but true, few traders ever learn how to discipline themselves no matter how many losses they take.

Even more amazing is that many traders are still convinced that their ticket to success is to find a better trading system. Actually, most traders will lose with any trading system no matter how well it tests or how promising it appears to be. A disciplined trader can be highly successful with a mediocre trading system, and a bad trader can be a failure with an otherwise outstanding trading system. Clearly, there is only a limited positive correlation between trading-system potential as revealed by historical testing and its actual performance in the hands of a trader. There is absolutely no doubt in my mind that the trader makes the system and not vice versa.

Now that the problem has been stated, the issue is how to remedy it. To suggest that I can provide the answers in several pages of text would be the height of sophistry. I can, however, address the subject with considerable authority given my years of trading experience and my intensive observations of how others trade. Traders throughout the world have told me of the benefits they have derived from my 1980 book, *The Investor's Quotient*, and from my 1988 book, *Beyond the Investor's Quotient*. My work with trading systems both as developer and trader has given me a unique perspective on the discipline problems that face all traders. Although my suggestions can be very helpful, they are not to be taken merely at face value. You will need to study and refine them to fit your trading style and your personality.

A Few Good Ways to Lose Money Trading the Futures Markets

E.L. Thorndike, the father of American learning psychology, noted that there are literally thousands of wrong behaviors and only relatively few right behaviors. His point was made in reference to the use of punishment as an aid to learning. While some new behaviors may be taught with punishment, the use of rewards for appropriate behaviors gets faster, better, and longer-lasting results.

Although there are many ways to lose money in the markets, there are only a few ways to make it—and even fewer ways to keep it. While traders collectively spend millions of dollars every year attending seminars and buying books, tapes, and trading systems, they focus little energy on learning behaviors to facilitate success. Why? Because the rules of trading systems, methods, and indicators are specific, often objective, and frequently require nothing more than rote memorization. In other words, they're easy to learn and easy to apply.

Behaviors that contribute to success, on the other hand, are often intangible, somewhat subjective, situation-relevant, and individual-dependent. No hard-and-fast rules apply to every trader. Frequently, traders are not in touch with the problems that require remediation. Not knowing what to change, they will surely be at a loss for techniques to help them make changes.

Perhaps my backdoor approach will be sufficiently unorthodox to get you started. Ignoring Thorndike and other outstanding behavioral psychologists, I'll tell you what you may be doing wrong. In so doing, I hope to break the monotony of do-this and do-that rules—ones often heard that somehow fail to find their way to the cerebral cortex. Here, then, are some good ways to lose money in the futures (and stock) markets.

Plunge Headlong into the Market without a Plan of Action

This is an excellent way to lose money and lose it quickly. Why make a plan anyway? If you trade without a plan, your chances of success are slim to none. You may be one of the lucky few who hits it big the first time, but the odds of doing so are minimal. Without a plan, you will find yourself buffeted by the winds of chance, the opinions of others, the persuasion of newsletters and advisors, the pandering of brokers, and the bias of the media. Your responses will be whimsical. But the greatest danger is that you will not learn anything from your behavior. If you are unaware of what you did wrong, the consequences of your actions will not be readily apparent to you. And you may run out of money before you learn your lessons.

But what exactly do I mean by a plan? Is it a trading system? A schedule? A set of rules? I define a trading plan as:

> **A system or set of indicators that will permit relatively objective evaluations of market entry and exit as well as risk management.**

This could mean that you are following a computerized trading system, signals from a chart book, a newsletter, astrology, a random-number generator, the I Ching, or your broker. Regardless of the source, the input must be treated as relatively unalterable and followed as closely and as often as possible. For some traders, I advise against rigid adherence to any system. Some traders cannot blindly follow a totally mechanical system. I suggest instead employing a relatively mechanical trade entry system and a more flexible exit system (to be discussed later on). In other words, I advise against rigidity, against inflexibility, and against blindly following any plan. However, to stray from a plan intelligently, you must have a plan at the outset.

There are various levels of adherence to a plan. Every trader must find his or her own level of comfort in deviating from that plan. Some traders will feel uncomfortable with only a minor deviation from the course, while others will be able to tolerate wide variances from their plans. You alone can determine the right formula by trial and error.

Read Many Publications, Watch the Television Business News, and Follow the Consensus of Opinion

This is a surefire way to get confused and lose money at the same time. I call this approach "Edsel trading," named after the infamous Edsel that was designed by a committee attempting to incorporate all of the changes and features recommended by experts and consumers alike. While the Edsel may have been well ahead of its time, it failed miserably as a product. When you attempt to trade on the basis of the consensus of opinion, you'll end up with an Edsel trading system, a system that seems like it should work but doesn't. In fact, my research with contrary opinion indicators strongly suggests that you are better off trading against majority opinion than with it. Futures trading is a loner's game. You must find a combination of indicators and tools that works for you—shut out as much outside influence as possible.

Add to Losing Positions to Average Your Cost

Here's a great method for losing your speculative capital. In fact, it works so well that many traders have virtually guaranteed themselves losses by following this time-tested strategy. The methodology is simple: Whenever a position goes against you, hold on to it and add to it repeatedly to lower your average cost. When the market eventually moves your way, you will come out ahead. The reasoning is very logical in a game where no margin is required and time is not important. But in futures, and particularly in futures options, time passed is money lost. Contracts expire, margin calls continue, and the trend most often continues in its existing direction. While you may be right in the long run, you will most likely be broke in the short run.

Take Your Profits Quickly and Ride Your Losses

This is another popular strategy among losers. To see why this approach is so popular, let's examine its psychology. Most traders are anxious. They are so worried about the ego-deflating experience of being wrong and losing money that when they have a profit, they are afraid it will not last. They are inclined to jump out of their profits quickly to get the gratification of knowing that they have banked the money and that the market cannot take it back. However, when there is a loss, things are quite different. Traders simply cannot admit to a loss. There is the perennial hope that things will eventually get better, that the market will turn around. And each small turnaround rewards the trader for hanging on. Unfortunately, it is often a classic case of one step forward and two steps back as the position continues to erode.

Start with Limited Capital and Attempt to Parlay It into a Fortune

This is the trader's utopian dream. The Horatio Alger story is still the image that inspires traders to take their shot at making it big in futures trading. Most traders begin with limited capital, seeking to hit the one big trade that will propel them to success. However, the odds of doing so are slim. The simple fact is this: The less you start with, the lower your odds of success. It's a matter of logic. If you're hoping to get on board that one big move, it may take 10 consecutive losers before the winner comes. By then your capital could easily be depleted, and you'll miss the move you were hoping for.

My advice: Be realistic. Begin with a good capital base. Be prepared for numerous small losses. Expect to be wrong 5, even 10, trades in a row before you hit a big trade. When you do hit a big one, don't get out too quick. Remember that the less you begin with, the less likely your chances of success.

Find a Trading System, Advisory Letter, or Money Manager That Has Performed Well and Latch On

Now here is another surefire way to lose your shirt. The time to go with a winner is when it has had a string of losses. Unfortunately, this is not the way most traders make their decisions. The temptation to go with a system or money manager is greatest when their performance has been outstanding, when they have attracted the most attention by their performance. I suggest that you find a good performer, wait until it has experienced a good-sized decline, and go with it. However, please note that your incentive to get on board will not be very high when the decline in performance is in process.

Quit Your Job, Withdraw Money from the Bank, Get a Computer, Subscribe to a Quote Service, and Begin Trading

I have seen more traders lose money this way than any other way. Futures trading is a profession. It takes time to learn the techniques, and it takes experience to implement those techniques successfully. There is no substitute for actual trading experience. It never ceases to amaze me how many doctors, lawyers, and engineers quit their otherwise stable and lucrative professions to take up trading. Even more amazing is the sad but true fact that these professionals think they can make money by taking a few courses or seminars, or by reading a few books. When their efforts meet with losses, they are surprised that they have failed. What they have failed to understand is that futures trading is not like being a doctor, lawyer, or engineer.

My advice is simple. Don't quit your job. Don't buy expensive quote equipment or computers. Don't fool yourself into thinking that the right system, the right computer, or the right broker will make you successful. Trial and error, experience, self-discipline, and consistency will make you more money than will expensive equipment.

Use Spreads to Avoid Losses

This may seem like a sophisticated strategy. In actuality, it's just another way of avoiding a loss until it gets big enough to cause serious pain. While there's nothing wrong with trading spreads as spreads, there's everything wrong with spreading a position to avoid a loss. The only thing this will do for you is to lock in the loss. Often both sides of the spread will work against you, and you will end up increasing your loss. The time to take your loss is when the time to take your loss has come; it's not time to spread the position to avoid a loss. When used appropriately, spreads are good vehicles that may be used very profitably. However, when used to avoid a loss, they can be deadly.

Pyramid Your Position as It Becomes Profitable

Pyramids are burial vaults. Unfortunately, many traders mistakenly believe that as a market moves in their favor, they must add successively larger numbers of contracts to capitalize on the move. What happens, of course, is that the pyramid is built upside down. These individuals will buy one unit at the start of a move, add two or three more at a higher price, and add five or six more at an even higher price. The pyramid becomes top-heavy, and the slightest change in trend will send it crashing to the ground along with the trader's profits.

If you're going to build a pyramid, build it with a sound base. Establish your largest position at the beginning of a move and add successively smaller numbers of units as the market moves in your favor. You will still have a good-sized position when the move comes to an end, and your average cost will be much better than if you had built the top-heavy pyramid. In spite of all we know about futures trading and all that has been written about the ill-advised procedure of the top-heavy pyramid, there are still traders who think this strategy will work for them; however, success is rare indeed.

Attempt to Pick Bottoms and Tops as Often as Possible

After all, the better your entry and the better your exit, the more money you stand to make. The reasoning sounds good, and if there were a good way to pick tops and bottoms with a high degree of accuracy, the reasoning would be correct. But tops and bottoms are elusive, and they are dangerous. Often a great deal of volatility is associated with tops and bottoms, making them hard to find and hard to stay with once they have been found.

Buy Futures Options to Limit Your Risk

This is a wonderful way to throw your money into the deep, dark hole. At first blush, this strategy seems just as logical as do many others. Joe Granville, stock market guru of the 1970s, used to say, "If it's obvious, then it's obviously wrong." This is especially true in futures options. In practice a vast majority of puts and calls expire worthless. To buy a call when you expect an uptrend or to buy a put when you expect a downtrend is often a waste of time, money, and commissions.

Options lose time value quickly. Your timing with options must be even better than it is with futures; it's a case of double jeopardy. You buy an option because you think you're buying time. You think that your timing need not be as precise as it is with futures because you can only lose your premium plus commissions when you buy options. This is the illusory aspect of the situation.

Professional futures traders who make money with options are most often sellers of options, since they know that most options expire worthless. They sell a deteriorating asset, and the odds are clearly in their favor. Thus, if you're going to trade futures options, do it in a professional way by using options strategies and by being an options seller rather than an options buyer. Unless you're willing to approach options in a professional way, don't even bother getting involved in this market.

How about Some Positive Suggestions?

Now that I have your attention, I will give you a few positive suggestions regarding trading discipline. Again, I will attempt to avoid standard recommendations.

Begin with a Simple Trading System.   My years of research have revealed one important thing: The simplest trading systems often work best. Yes, I know all about the claims and the hypothetical performance records. I know all about the optimized systems and the black box systems and the virtues of artificial intelligence. But I keep coming back to the same conclusion as a result of my research: Simple systems work best. Once you have experienced profits using a simple method, you can experiment with complex systems and decide for yourself.

Be Independent, Isolate Yourself, and Remain Pure.   The trader's mind is a delicate machine. It is easily affected by the many inputs that daily impinge on the decision-making process. The futures market thrives on opinions, mass psychology, emotion, news, and rumors. The less you hear, the better off you'll be.

Most systems are correct between 50 and 65 percent of the time; however, even this 15 percent margin above chance occurrence is obviously not a large margin of safety. By allowing the input of others to affect you, this margin may be neutralized and you will lose your advantage. The ability to clearly see the markets is a great asset.

Don't Read the Market News.   If you subscribe to one of the two daily U.S. financial papers, do so for technical data only. The news reports and opinions of the reporting staff are poison unless, of course, you can train yourself to do the opposite of what the majority recommends.

Don't Get More than Two Advisory Services.   Actually, you're better off with one or none. If you get one service, follow it as closely as you can. Don't pick and choose from among its recommendations. Follow all recommendations or follow none. Most traders pick and choose wrong.

Use a Discount Broker.   Unless you do business with a broker who is also your advisor, use a discount broker who will not bother you with opinions or pressure you with trading ideas. If you decide on a broker who will also advise you, make sure it is one with considerable experience who is not in business for the simple purpose of generating commissions. Although difficult to find, such brokers are definitely out there.

Don't Discuss Your Trades with Anyone.   Discussing your trades, signals, methods, or indicators with other traders only infects them with your ideas and you with theirs. Confusion will be the end result.

Don't Read Popular Trading Magazines.   Most are full of ideas that don't work. If you have arrived at your goal of self-discipline, read all you want. Otherwise, avoid trading.

Don't Discuss the Markets with Friends.   Your opinions are not important to friends and their opinions are not important to you. In stating your opinions, you will reinforce them to yourself, and you will be inclined to hold on to them in spite of what your system may say.

Begin with Sufficient Capital, Trade Small Positions, and Diversify Your Trading. Attempt to spread your risk over several different markets. Avoid the lure of large positions. The need to trade large positions essentially stems from ego and feelings of inadequacy. Many people need to compensate for negative self-concepts by asserting their power in the markets. They attempt to prove their machismo by being aggressive, trading large positions, taking chances, and asserting their independence. You will be much better off beginning as a small fish in a big pond who seeks small, reliable market moves as opposed to large, unreliable moves. Size creates problems. It's not the size of your position that's important, but how you trade your position that will make you a winner or a loser. Once you have learned how to trade, you can tackle the problems that come with large positions.

Change Your Perception of the Market. That's easier said than done! All organisms are captives of their perceptions. If you see the market as an adversary, you will approach it as a soldier approaches combat. If, however, you perceive the market as a vehicle that you must learn to operate, you will learn how to operate it to your advantage. Your attitude about the market will shape the way you trade. It is far easier to go with the flow of the market than it is to fight the trend.

Do Your Homework. If you have settled on a particular trading system or method, you must be strictly dedicated to it. If you do not keep your work up to date, you will miss most market moves.

Be Prepared for Numerous Consecutive Losses. One of the most frustrating, anxiety-provoking things a trader can experience is a string of numerous consecutive losses. These are the most difficult times for futures traders. They cause errors, inconsistency, lack of discipline, and the search for new systems. If you are prepared for the worst before it happens, you will be able to cope with it when it actually does happen. And, believe me, it will!

Summary

The study of human emotion provides us with the big picture of trading. If we can identify where human emotion is taking the rest of the trading community without becoming influenced by it, we will know that the markets will soon be moving in the opposite direction and profit by that knowledge. This distance from the emotions of others, however, requires us to be able to distance ourselves from our own emotions.

Following our rational thoughts means fighting the powerful current going in the opposite direction. This constant internal battle requires enormous energy and commitment. Nevertheless, the destination for the battle-scarred trader who is willing to engage in this effort is the land of successful trading. Given the emotions that run rampant in day trading, my rules are very important.

Additionally, there are, to be sure, many more rules that apply to successful day trading. Some of the ones included in this chapter may not be universally applicable, and some rules that are needed for individual traders may not have been included. For that reason, you would benefit immensely from a formulation of your own trading rules because you, alone, are the best judge of what you need. To do this, however, you must first become totally aware of your needs, assets, liabilities, skills, and goals. In the meantime, study the ones I have included and see how they fit.

10

What Markets to Day Trade?

The reasonable man adapts himself to the world; the unreasonable one persists in trying to adapt the world to himself. Therefore all progress depends on the unreasonable man.
SHELLEY

In order for the day trader to succeed, it will be very important to trade markets that have two essential characteristics: They must be actively traded markets, and they must have fairly large daily trading ranges. In other words, part of the formula for success as a day trader is knowing which markets to trade. Essentially, the day trader must restrict his or her trading to markets that have high volatility. Although these markets that are best suited for day trading will not always remain constant, there are ways the trader may ascertain which markets are the best ones to trade at any given point in time.

Here are some guidelines to use in selecting which markets are ideally suited for the purpose of day trading. You will note that I essentially use two parameters: trading volume and volatility.

Trading Volume

The first consideration of the day trader should be the number of contracts that are traded daily. In some cases it will be very clear which markets are the most active. Markets such as the currencies, interest rate futures, and stock index futures will likely remain among the most active for many years to come. However, from time to time as a result of changes in fundamental market conditions, various markets may become more or less active. In the event of drought, for example, the grain and soybean complex markets would become highly active and therefore suitable for day trading. Some markets such as orange juice futures that are normally inactive can become heavily traded during periods of frost and freeze. Such situations when they arise will require that you use your best judgment as to whether day trades are feasible at that time. Ultimately it will always be up to the individual trader to determine whether a market has sufficient trading volume for the purpose of day trading.

In order to assist you in making your decision about which markets to day trade and which markets to avoid in day trading, this section will provide a number of guidelines. Note that none of these are written in stone. Unfortunately, there will always be some degree of judgment that may be involved in making the ultimate decision as to which markets should be traded. Determining a priori all circumstances and conditions that may arise in the future is impossible. Therefore, experience will truly be the best teacher in the final analysis.

In terms of trading volume it's always best to look at the number of contracts actually traded in the contract month that you wish to trade. Please note that the individual number of contracts traded for a particular delivery month is significantly different than the total volume traded for the entire commodity. Treasury bond futures, for example, may show a total volume of 847,000 contracts traded on a particular day; however, the actual volume in the active or nearby contract month may only be 200,112 contracts. While this example illustrates the significant difference between total volume and actual volume for the contract month, the situation in this case would clearly make a lead contract month suitable for day trading. In another situation, however, the lead contract month may not show sufficient trading volume, since most of the activity may be occurring in the back months.

As a general guideline I prefer to day trade markets that have a minimum of 10,000 contracts traded daily in the lead months. Please note that this is a general guideline. In some situations such as coffee futures (as of this writing), trading volume does not meet this minimum criterion; however, the market is still reasonably suited for day trading, provided one follows specific guidelines regarding the use of order entry that may minimize possibly deleterious effects of low trading volume.

Clearly, the best markets to day trade will not always be the same period. As of this writing (1998), the most active and the most readily day traded futures markets based on trading volume alone are as follows:

- S&P 500
- Treasury bonds
- Crude oil
- Heating oil
- Swiss franc
- Deutsche mark
- British pound
- Japanese yen
- Soybeans
- Coffee

Please note that I have included coffee here in spite of the fact that trading volume does not usually meet the minimum criteria I have indicated above. My reason for including coffee is because it is a market with considerable volatility a vast majority of the time. In this case I am making a decision to place volatility ahead of trading volume.

You may find it interesting to know that the opposite situation occurs in Eurodollar futures. This market trades very heavily in terms of overall trading volume; however, the intraday moves are relatively small most of the time. This market is, therefore, not suitable for the purpose of day trading. Eurodollar futures are, in fact, one of the most actively traded markets in terms of trading volume. We "outside" traders, by which I mean the off-the-floor traders, cannot successfully day trade this market. And this brings us to our second criterion for selecting markets to day trade.

Volatility

The second important consideration in determining which markets to day trade is volatility. Not all traders think of volatility in the same operational way as I do. For the purposes of this discussion, I consider *volatility* to mean "large trading range" on any given day. Preferably, the market you are considering for day trading should have, at the very minimum, a recent history of fairly large trading ranges. Given that dollar values for different markets are based on contract specifications and tick value, the best way to determine volatility is to convert the daily trading range into dollars, rather than to make comparisons based on points.

Here are a few examples that will illustrate my point about volatility very clearly. First, let's consider the example of Eurodollar futures. Assume that the market trades in a range of 20 points in 1 day. In this example, a range of 20 points in 1 day multiplied by 25 dollars per point equals $500. Deducting the cost of commissions, assuming slippage on entry and exit, the bottom-line or net profit, assuming one could capture most of the daily trading range, might only be 15 ticks. The end result would be a net profit of only $375. Given that Eurodollar futures' trading range is considerably less than 20 points, you can see that it is unfeasible to day trade the Eurodollar futures market unless you are a floor broker.

On the other hand, consider the case of Treasury bond futures. The average daily trading range in this market is frequently 25 ticks. At approximately $32 per tick, a 25-tick daily trading range is approximately $900. This is a very respectable trading range for day traders and is certainly much more palatable and workable than the $375 trading range given in the Eurodollar example above.

The quintessence of all day-trading markets at the time this book is being written is, of course, the S&P 500. Rarely a day goes by without S&P trading in a range of less than 600 points. This represents a sizable dollar amount. Clearly the S&P 500 futures market is the preeminent day traders market. The good news is that S&P 500 futures are not only volatile but also show large trading volume each day. It is this combination that makes the S&P 500 market ideal for day traders.

The Double-Edged Sword

As you can clearly see, the ideal market for day traders is the market that has both range and volatility. Both elements must be present in sufficient degree in order to make day trading viable as well as potentially profitable. The successful day trader, however, must always bear in mind that volatility and trading volume constitute a double-edged sword. While they help create day-trading opportunities, they are also responsible for the wide trading swings that frequently cause day traders to take losses. Volatile markets "giveth and taketh away." Just as a volatile market will help the day trader by presenting opportunities, volatility will also create price swings that have the potential to cause losses by hitting your stop losses.

Changing Conditions

I indicated earlier that day-trading opportunities may change over time as a function of different conditions, fundamental and/or political, that may arise from time to time. Among the conditions that may create trading opportunities in relatively quiet markets are such things as weather, political events, armed conflict, and, of course, changes in fundamental economic conditions. Consider the following examples:

Orange Juice. This is a market that normally trades very lightly. Certain events—frost and freeze scares, for example—can result in a substantial increase in both market volatility as well as trading volume. When this happens, the normally quiet OJ market becomes very active—even to the extent that it can be used for the purpose of day trading. In such situations the experienced day trader will watch closely for signs that conditions are about to change, resulting in a return to the usually thin market conditions.

Coffee. The coffee market has for many years been subject not only to significant price moves based on weather, but it has also been a highly political market, subject many times to the actions of coffee cartels. When such conditions have arisen, coffee futures have become highly volatile, frequently making moves of well over 500 points per day. At $375 per 100 points, day trading coffee futures is quite viable. On the other hand, when the news backdrop in coffee futures is rather tame, the 100- or 200-point range makes this market unsuitable for day trading.

Sugar. Typically the sugar market trades in a range of approximately 20 points per day. Since the tick value of sugar futures is

$11.20, a 20-tick trading range per day is insufficient for day traders. Hence, under normal conditions the sugar market is not recommended for day trading. Weather factors, production fundamentals, demand, and inflationary pressures can cause the daily trading range of sugar futures to expand markedly. Under such circumstances the daily trading range can increase to as much as 60 points per day. Even under such conditions, the daily trading range of sugar is unlikely to exceed $1000. Therefore, it is reasonably safe to assume that the day trader will rarely, if ever, day trade sugar futures.

Can Commodity Spreads Be Day Traded?

A topic that has received very little attention in the past is the use of commodity spreads. Over the years I have discovered that only a few traders truly understand spreads. In fact, I have found that even those traders who do understand spreads have difficulty placing spread orders, lacking understanding of the technical aspects of spread trading and the knowledge that is required to trade spreads. This is truly unfortunate, since I consider commodity spread trading to be one of the highest-probability and most reliable aspects of the futures trading.

Experienced commodity traders are well aware that most commodity spreads have a strong underlying seasonal basis. It is the strong seasonal basis of most commodity spreads that makes them viable position trading markets. On an intraday basis, however, seasonality does not apply. Hence, no matter how strong a seasonal tendency may be, it will not be applicable for the purpose of day trading. The question is "Can spread be traded on intraday bases using some of the technical tools contained in this book?" In order to answer this question, we must first determine whether the spreads we wish to day trade meet the two criteria we have already discussed in this chapter. Specifically, is the spread volatile and does the spread have sufficient trading volume to permit viable and effective day trading?

The first issue, volatility, is easily answered by examining the entry day-trading range of the area's spreads. In so doing we find that there are certain spreads that appear to meet the volatility prerequisite for day trading. At the time of this writing, a number of currency, interest rate, and grain/soybean complex spreads meet this criterion. Remember that the ideal markets for day trading spreads will change over time. Please refer to my discussion above for details regarding such changes.

The issue of trading volume, which is also important in determining what markets to day trade, is not easily determined for spreads. Since a commodity spread is not considered a countable trade in terms of volume statistics, it is impossible to know for certain how many commodity spreads of a given type are being traded. As a general rule, it is not unreasonable to assume that large trading volume in the underlying individual contract month or markets will correlate strongly with large trading volume in the spread. Ultimately, however, the individual trader will need to decide which spreads to trade.

Recommended Spreads for Day Trading

Here is a list of spreads that are currently active and therefore viable for day trading. Please note that these spreads will not always be sufficiently active for the purposes of day trading.

The Swiss Franc versus D-Mark Spread. This has been a reasonably active spread for many years. Since the relationship between the Swiss franc and the Deutsche mark is not only a closely watched spread but also a very active one, it is quite suitable for the purposes of the day trader. Depending upon the fundamental relationship between the two markets at any given point in time, this spread can be relatively tame or highly volatile. I suggest using the same price range and volume criteria in order to evaluate this spread.

The Swiss Franc versus Japanese Yen Spread. This spread has also enjoyed a lengthy history of volatility, as well as considerable trading volume. It is therefore highly suitable for day trading. A word of caution is strongly recommended at this point. Because of the volatility in this spread, I urge you to use specific price orders for entry and exit. By using specific orders, you can avoid considerable problems, as well as losses and poor price executions.

The Swiss Franc versus British Pound Spread. This spread has not been as volatile as the two previously described. Although there have been times during which this spread has been extremely volatile, there have also been periods of relative dormancy. It is therefore imperative that you trade this spread only during times of high volume as well as volatility. Use the factors previously cited in order to evaluate these conditions. As in the case of most spreads, I strongly recommend using specific place orders for entry and exit.

Soybeans versus Corn Spread.   Here is yet another spread that tends to alternate between periods of volatility and periods of relative dormancy. Typically, the times during which this spread is sufficiently active for trading are when weather conditions during the planting season and the harvest season affect crop development. Carefully consider and evaluate the trading range in this spread before you determine whether to day trade it.

Wheat versus Corn Spread.   As in the case of the soybean versus corn spread, the wheat versus corn spread also has periods of relative quiet and relative volatility. These are most often associated with fundamental conditions such as weather, harvest, planting, and import/export business. Do not rule this spread out as a viable day-trading vehicle, but be certain to trade it only when both markets are volatile.

Energy Spreads.   In addition to the spreads cited above, the energy spreads tend to be good vehicles for day trading. In particular, heating oil versus crude oil, unleaded gas versus heating oil, unleaded gas versus crude oil, and natural gas versus any of the petroleum complex markets tend to be volatile spreads.

Summary

This chapter discussed a number of guidelines that should be used in determining which markets to day trade. Specific rules were given. The possibility of day trading spreads was also discussed in detail. I indicated that there are a number of spreads that can be day traded. I have not addressed technical tools for the purpose of day trading spreads. These are discussed in other chapters.

11

Closings and Openings

Of all the things I have learned about futures trading, the most important is that markets form patterns. The future direction of a market is often, but not always, discernible from the study of its patterns. And there are many patterns one can study—cyclical patterns, seasonal patterns, open interest and volume patterns, indicator patterns, price structure patterns, point-and-figure patterns, Japanese candlestick patterns, chart patterns, and more. Of these, many are worthless or specious. But there are a few worth knowing, worth studying, and worth trading.

Of all patterns, the most important and reliable I have found are based upon combinations and variations of the four important price variables each day: the opening price, the closing price, the high price, and the low price. By studying these, we can develop indicators that will be especially beneficial not only from the standpoint of predictability but, moreover, from the standpoint of profitability.

High/Low/Close Relationships

As an example of a price pattern that can occur within the course of a day, consider the relationship between the high price, the low price, and the closing price of the day. A market that ends the day close to its high of the day is one that is clearly in control of the buyers. Buyers have overpowered sellers, bidding prices higher, and as a result, the closing price of the day is near the high of the day.

A market that closes close to its low of the day is in control of the bears. The selling pressure of the bears has been enough to push prices lower and lower until they end the day near their low. In such a case, the bears are in control, overpowering the buying power of the bulls.

A market that consistently closes close to its high of the day, day after day, is a market that is clearly being controlled by the bulls, whereas a market that consistently closes close to its low of the day, day after day, is a market that is clearly bearish. The same relation-

Figure 11-1. Closing near highs on daily price chart. Note how the market surged higher following 3 days on which the closing price was very near the high price of the day.

ship applies on an intraday basis using shorter time lengths than a day. As an example, consider the daily price chart of T-bond futures (Figure 11-1). This illustration shows how a strong bullish move develops subsequent to three daily price bars where the ending price (close) is near the high of the daily time frame. Figure 11-2 shows the opposite situation. Note how the daily crude oil futures chart shows a strong decline subsequent to three daily price bars where the ending price (close) is near the low of the daily time frame. Note also that for the duration of the decline, many of the daily price bars show a close near the low of the bar. This is typical of bear trends, while the reverse is typical of bull trends.

Figures 11-3 and 11-4 illustrate this relationship on intraday charts of different time lengths. As you can see, the same basic relationships hold true on an intraday time frame.

Although the close-near-high or close-near-low relationship is a valuable one, there are others that may prove even more valuable. In fact, a number of such relationships may be combined in order to yield more reliable results.

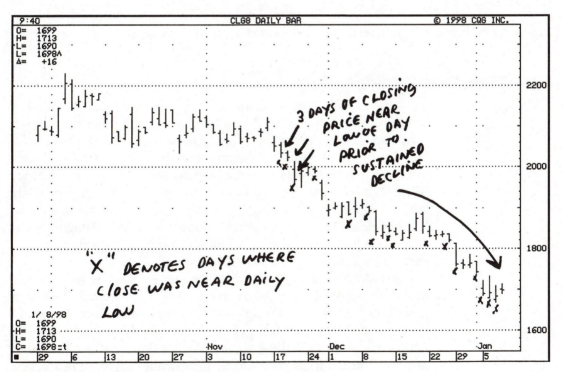

Figure 11-2. Closing near lows on daily price chart.

Figure 11-3. Closings near price bar highs on intraday 30-minute chart.

Open/Close Relationships

Yet another, and, I believe, more important relationship is that of the close versus the open. A market that closes higher than where it has opened is one that has likely been under accumulation for the day or for the given time frame. A market that closes lower than where it opened is one that is likely the subject of persistency selling. A consistent close below opens is considered bearish, while a consistent close above opens is considered bullish. A market that closes higher than where it opens and near the high of the day is one that I consider very bullish, and vice versa for a market that closes near its lows and below its open.

Figure 11-5 illustrates the close-greater-than-open relationship on a daily price chart. As you can see, closing above the opening is typical of bull trends. Figure 11-6 illustrates the opposite condition. Closing below the open is characteristic of bear trends. Although these two illustrations depict daily price charts, the same relationship is true on all time-frame levels. Figure 11-7 shows these relationships on an intraday chart.

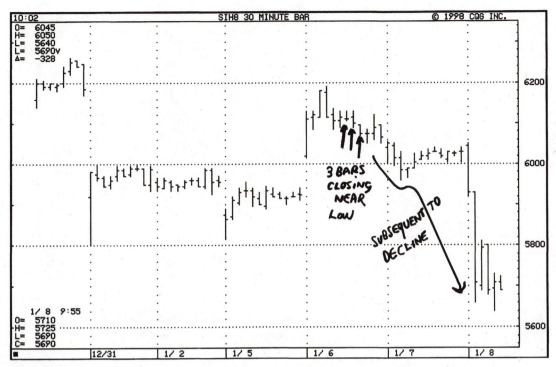

Figure 11-4. Closings near price bar lows on intraday 30-minute chart.

Developing a Trading System on the Open versus Close Relationship

Knowing that such relationships are important and that they tend to precede rallies and declines, is there a way in which they may be used for day trading? Based on my work I feel that there is. The method that I have developed based on the open versus close/open relationships is called COR. Here is a synopsis of how it works.

- Following x consecutive price bars where the close is greater than the open, a *buy* signal is triggered and a long position initiated on the opening of the next price bar.
- Following x consecutive price bars where the close is less than the open, a *sell* signal is triggered and a short position initiated on the opening of the next price bar.
- If there is a current position based on a previous signal, it is reversed and a profit or loss is taken.

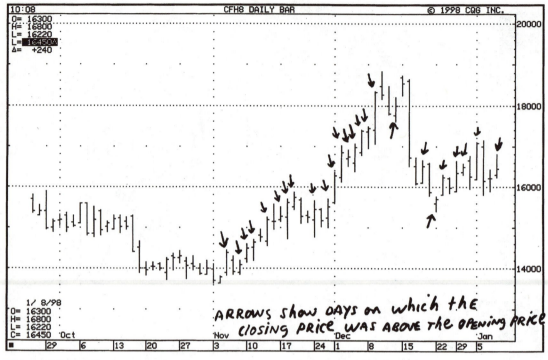

Figure 11-5. Closings greater than openings on a daily price chart.

- An initial stop loss (money management stop) is used.
- When a given profit amount has been reached (floor amount), then a trailing stop loss is used. The trailing stop loss is a given percentage of the open profit as measured from an open profit peak. In other words, the market must retrace gains from an open profit peak by a certain amount before the trade is stopped out.
- If the stop is hit, the trade is closed out and no new position is entered until the next signal.
- A profit is taken either by being stopped out or by exit on the *n*th profitable opening.
- If neither of these conditions is met, then you exit on the close of the same day (MOC).

As you can see, this approach provides several alternatives, all ideally suited for the day trader. It provides all the necessary elements. When programmed on a daily live data feed, the software,

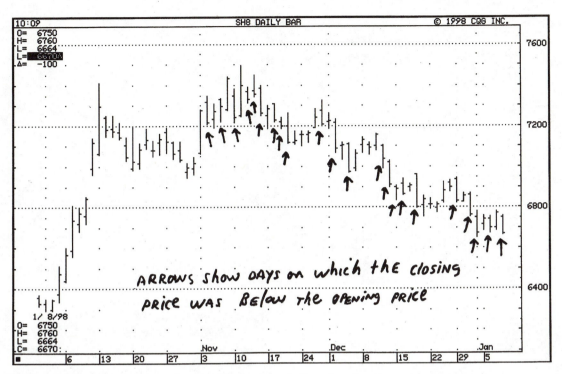

Figure 11-6. Closings less than openings on a daily price chart.

such as Omega TradeStation™, will automatically generate the entry and exit points for you based on the input parameters.

Historical Records

Using tick-by-tick data, I back-tested the COR. My work indicated that the method works best on 20-minute price bars. I back-tested approximately 569 trades in three different yearly time frames, as shown by the historical records in Figures 11-9 through 11-12. Figure 11-8 shows how the trades appear on an intraday chart. See my notations.

The best market for this approach is S&P futures, although the method can be adapted for use in any active market that is suitable for day trading. The parameters used for each of the tests are listed on the accompanying historical printouts. You will note the following general conclusions based on the above system test results:

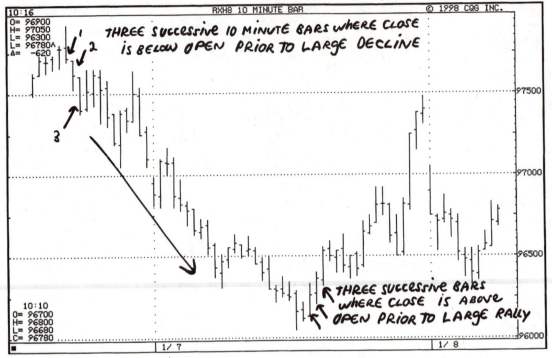

Figure 11-7. Open greater than close and open less than close on intraday chart.

- The usual long-entry successive bars is 3–4, while the usual short-entry bars is longer, at about 5–8. This is a characteristic of bull markets. In a bull market, valid sell signals tend to occur after a longer string of closes below opens because the underlying or secular market trend is bullish. Reactions to the downside tend to recover quickly, which means that a shorter number of bars that show closes below opens will likely yield false signals.

- The initial stop loss amount is, of course, a function of market volatility. The very volatile S&P market of 1997 required a very large initial stop loss, whereas the relatively tame S&P market of 1990 required a smaller initial stop loss. The 1997 stop loss was about four times the size of the 1990 stop loss. Please note that in *all* day trading it is important to give the market plenty of room by using a larger stop loss as opposed to a smaller stop loss. Unfortunately, this goes against the grain of many traders who mistakenly think that small stops are the best way to trade profitably.

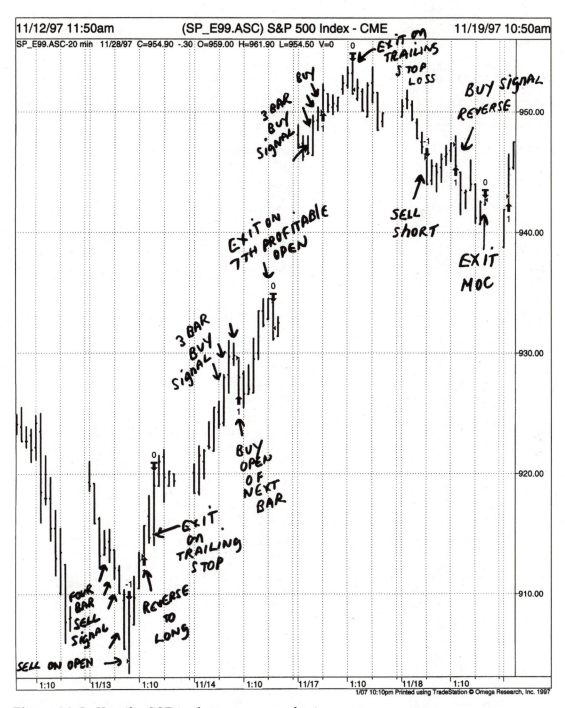

Figure 11-8. How the COR trades appear on a chart.

SP_E99.ASC-20 min   01/10/97 - 11/28/97

Performance Summary: All Trades

Total net profit	$ 111150.00	Open position P/L	$ 0.00
Gross profit	$ 323950.00	Gross loss	$-212800.00
Total # of trades	300	Percent profitable	61%
Number winning trades	182	Number losing trades	118
Largest winning trade	$ 12925.00	Largest losing trade	$ -5875.00
Average winning trade	$ 1779.95	Average losing trade	$ -1803.39
Ratio avg win/avg loss	0.99	Avg trade(win & loss)	$ 370.50
Max consec. winners	10	Max consec. losers	5
Avg # bars in winners	6	Avg # bars in losers	5
Max intraday drawdown	$ -26100.00		
Profit factor	1.52	Max # contracts held	1
Account size required	$ 26100.00	Return on account	426%

- -

Performance Summary: Long Trades

Total net profit	$ 38650.00	Open position P/L	$ 0.00
Gross profit	$ 200625.00	Gross loss	$-161975.00
Total # of trades	203	Percent profitable	61%
Number winning trades	124	Number losing trades	79
Largest winning trade	$ 7425.00	Largest losing trade	$ -5875.00
Average winning trade	$ 1617.94	Average losing trade	$ -2050.32
Ratio avg win/avg loss	0.79	Avg trade(win & loss)	$ 190.39
Max consec. winners	8	Max consec. losers	6
Avg # bars in winners	6	Avg # bars in losers	6
Max intraday drawdown	$ -40600.00		
Profit factor	1.24	Max # contracts held	1
Account size required	$ 40600.00	Return on account	95%

- -

Performance Summary: Short Trades

Total net profit	$ 72500.00	Open position P/L	$ 0.00
Gross profit	$ 123325.00	Gross loss	$ -50825.00
Total # of trades	97	Percent profitable	60%
Number winning trades	58	Number losing trades	39
Largest winning trade	$ 12925.00	Largest losing trade	$ -4425.00
Average winning trade	$ 2126.29	Average losing trade	$ -1303.21
Ratio avg win/avg loss	1.63	Avg trade(win & loss)	$ 747.42
Max consec. winners	6	Max consec. losers	4
Avg # bars in winners	5	Avg # bars in losers	3
Max intraday drawdown	$ -8000.00		
Profit factor	2.43	Max # contracts held	1
Account size required	$ 8000.00	Return on account	906%

Figure 11-9. Historical record COR in S&P from 1/10/97 through 11/28/97. Parameters: Long entry—3 bars close > open. Short entry—4 bars close < open. Initial stop loss is $5400. Floor amount is $1700. Trailing stop is 50%. Exit seventh profitable open or MOC.

```
SP_E99.ASC-20 min    01/11/96 - 11/27/96
```

Performance Summary: All Trades

Total net profit	$	34250.00	Open position P/L	$ 0.00
Gross profit	$	54775.00	Gross loss	$ -20525.00
Total # of trades		80	Percent profitable	66%
Number winning trades		53	Number losing trades	27
Largest winning trade	$	5950.00	Largest losing trade	$ -1275.00
Average winning trade	$	1033.49	Average losing trade	$ -760.19
Ratio avg win/avg loss		1.36	Avg trade(win & loss)	$ 428.13
Max consec. winners		9	Max consec. losers	3
Avg # bars in winners		6	Avg # bars in losers	5
Max intraday drawdown	$	-3375.00		
Profit factor		2.67	Max # contracts held	1
Account size required	$	3375.00	Return on account	1015%

— — · — · — · — — · — — · — · — · — — · — — · — · — · — — · — · · — — ·

Performance Summary: Long Trades

Total net profit	$	27925.00	Open position P/L	$ 0.00
Gross profit	$	41075.00	Gross loss	$ -13150.00
Total # of trades		58	Percent profitable	66%
Number winning trades		38	Number losing trades	20
Largest winning trade	$	5950.00	Largest losing trade	$ -1275.00
Average winning trade	$	1080.92	Average losing trade	$ -657.50
Ratio avg win/avg loss		1.64	Avg trade(win & loss)	$ 481.47
Max consec. winners		7	Max consec. losers	3
Avg # bars in winners		7	Avg # bars in losers	4
Max intraday drawdown	$	-3175.00		
Profit factor		3.12	Max # contracts held	1
Account size required	$	3175.00	Return on account	880%

— — · — · — · — — · — — · — · — · — — · — — · — · — · — — · — · · — — ·

Performance Summary: Short Trades

Total net profit	$	6325.00	Open position P/L	$ 0.00
Gross profit	$	13700.00	Gross loss	$ -7375.00
Total # of trades		22	Percent profitable	68%
Number winning trades		15	Number losing trades	7
Largest winning trade	$	2325.00	Largest losing trade	$ -1275.00
Average winning trade	$	913.33	Average losing trade	$ -1053.57
Ratio avg win/avg loss		0.87	Avg trade(win & loss)	$ 287.50
Max consec. winners		4	Max consec. losers	2
Avg # bars in winners		5	Avg # bars in losers	7
Max intraday drawdown	$	-2425.00		
Profit factor		1.86	Max # contracts held	1
Account size required	$	2425.00	Return on account	261%

Figure 11-10. Historical record COR in S&P from 1/11/96 through 11/27/96. Parameters: Long entry—5 bars close > open. Short entry—6 bars close < open. Initial stop loss is $1200. Floor amount is $1100. Trailing stop is 40%. Exit tenth profitable open or MOC.

Performance Summary: All Trades

Total net profit	$ 97775.00	Open position P/L	$ 0.00
Gross profit	$ 236500.00	Gross loss	$-138725.00
Total # of trades	268	Percent profitable	76%
Number winning trades	205	Number losing trades	63
Largest winning trade	$ 5550.00	Largest losing trade	$ -4825.00
Average winning trade	$ 1153.66	Average losing trade	$ -2201.98
Ratio avg win/avg loss	0.52	Avg trade(win & loss)	$ 364.83
Max consec. winners	13	Max consec. losers	2
Avg # bars in winners	5	Avg # bars in losers	8
Max intraday drawdown	$ -12950.00		
Profit factor	1.70	Max # contracts held	1
Account size required	$ 12950.00	Return on account	755%

Performance Summary: Long Trades

Total net profit	$ 97500.00	Open position P/L	$ 0.00
Gross profit	$ 180875.00	Gross loss	$ -83375.00
Total # of trades	196	Percent profitable	81%
Number winning trades	158	Number losing trades	38
Largest winning trade	$ 5550.00	Largest losing trade	$ -4825.00
Average winning trade	$ 1144.78	Average losing trade	$ -2194.08
Ratio avg win/avg loss	0.52	Avg trade(win & loss)	$ 497.45
Max consec. winners	14	Max consec. losers	3
Avg # bars in winners	5	Avg # bars in losers	9
Max intraday drawdown	$ -11275.00		
Profit factor	2.17	Max # contracts held	1
Account size required	$ 11275.00	Return on account	865%

Performance Summary: Short Trades

Total net profit	$ 275.00	Open position P/L	$ 0.00
Gross profit	$ 55625.00	Gross loss	$ -55350.00
Total # of trades	72	Percent profitable	65%
Number winning trades	47	Number losing trades	25
Largest winning trade	$ 4200.00	Largest losing trade	$ -3975.00
Average winning trade	$ 1183.51	Average losing trade	$ -2214.00
Ratio avg win/avg loss	0.53	Avg trade(win & loss)	$ 3.82
Max consec. winners	8	Max consec. losers	3
Avg # bars in winners	4	Avg # bars in losers	8
Max intraday drawdown	$ -15475.00		
Profit factor	1.00	Max # contracts held	1
Account size required	$ 15475.00	Return on account	2%

Figure 11-11. Historical record COR in S&P from 11/03/95 through 11/28/97. Parameters: Long entry—4 bars close > open. Short entry—5 bars close < open. Initial stop loss is $3300. Floor is $800. Trailing stop loss is 50%. Exit third profitable open or MOC.

- The floor amount is relatively small in all cases. In other words, for this system to make money you must begin using a trailing stop as soon as you have a few hundred points of profit, since it is not uncommon for S&P futures to trade in a large range, at times taking away all of your open profit.

- The trailing stop loss percentage is applied to the floor amount. In most cases, it has run about 50 percent, although in more volatile markets you must be willing to give back a few more dollars given the wide intraday price swings.

- Exit on the *n*th profitable opening is an excellent strategy. In most cases, the seventh through the tenth profitable opening or MOC (whichever comes first) is the best strategy.

- Percentage accuracy has run from about 61 percent to a high of 76 percent over the time frames tested.

- The average trade in all cases is very respectable for a day trade, while drawdown is reasonable for S&P futures.

Variation on the Theme

As a slight deviation from the COR method, consider *not* exiting at the end of the day. I realize that if you do this, then the COR method will no longer be a day-trading method; however, it may yield considerably more profits and higher accuracy. As a case in point, consider the historical record shown in Figure 11-13. This report shows what happens when the COR trade is *not* closed out at the end of the day. Instead, the trade is held until the twentieth profitable open, or until it is stopped out or reversed by an opposite signal. As you can see, there is a dramatic improvement in results and in accuracy.

Compare the historical results here with those covering the same time span but with exit MOC or within the day on a stop (Figure 11-12), trailing stop loss, or the tenth profitable opening. The average profit per trade increases from $293 to over $638, while the accuracy increases from 67 percent to 77 percent. The total number of trades decreases because positions are held for a longer period of time, but the total net profit increases substantially.

This is a strong testimonial to the value of the method, but it also suggests that the day trader may, at times, wish to hold a position in the expectation of a larger average profit. One way to "have your profit and keep it too" is to trade multiple units (i.e., several contracts), taking day trade profits on one unit while hold-

```
SP_E99.ASC-20 min   01/11/90 - 11/28/90
```
Performance Summary: All Trades

Total net profit	$ 29100.00	Open position P/L	$ 0.00
Gross profit	$ 48450.00	Gross loss	$ -19350.00
Total # of trades	99	Percent profitable	67%
Number winning trades	66	Number losing trades	33
Largest winning trade	$ 2400.00	Largest losing trade	$ -1875.00
Average winning trade	$ 734.09	Average losing trade	$ -586.36
Ratio avg win/avg loss	1.25	Avg trade(win & loss)	$ 293.94
Max consec. winners	9	Max consec. losers	4
Avg # bars in winners	8	Avg # bars in losers	8
Max intraday drawdown	$ -3275.00		
Profit factor	2.50	Max # contracts held	1
Account size required	$ 3275.00	Return on account	889%

Performance Summary: Long Trades

Total net profit	$ 28350.00	Open position P/L	$ 0.00
Gross profit	$ 46600.00	Gross loss	$ -18250.00
Total # of trades	97	Percent profitable	67%
Number winning trades	65	Number losing trades	32
Largest winning trade	$ 2400.00	Largest losing trade	$ -1875.00
Average winning trade	$ 716.92	Average losing trade	$ -570.31
Ratio avg win/avg loss	1.26	Avg trade(win & loss)	$ 292.27
Max consec. winners	9	Max consec. losers	4
Avg # bars in winners	8	Avg # bars in losers	8
Max intraday drawdown	$ -3275.00		
Profit factor	2.55	Max # contracts held	1
Account size required	$ 3275.00	Return on account	866%

Performance Summary: Short Trades

Total net profit	$ 750.00	Open position P/L	$ 0.00
Gross profit	$ 1850.00	Gross loss	$ -1100.00
Total # of trades	2	Percent profitable	50%
Number winning trades	1	Number losing trades	1
Largest winning trade	$ 1850.00	Largest losing trade	$ -1100.00
Average winning trade	$ 1850.00	Average losing trade	$ -1100.00
Ratio avg win/avg loss	1.68	Avg trade(win & loss)	$ 375.00
Max consec. winners	1	Max consec. losers	1
Avg # bars in winners	12	Avg # bars in losers	13
Max intraday drawdown	$ -1475.00		
Profit factor	1.68	Max # contracts held	1
Account size required	$ 1475.00	Return on account	51%

Figure 11-12. Historical record COR in S&P from 1/11/90 through 11/28/90. Parameters: Long entry—4 bars close > open. Short entry—8 bars close < open. Initial stop loss is $1800. Floor is $900. Trailing stop loss is 50%. Exit tenth profitable open or MOC.

jb.3cho SP_E99.ASC-20 min   01/11/90 - 11/28/90

Performance Summary: All Trades

Total net profit	$ 47900.00	Open position P/L	$	0.00
Gross profit	$ 72750.00	Gross loss	$	-24850.00
Total # of trades	75	Percent profitable		77%
Number winning trades	58	Number losing trades		17
Largest winning trade	$ 7350.00	Largest losing trade	$	-2350.00
Average winning trade	$ 1254.31	Average losing trade	$	-1461.76
Ratio avg win/avg loss	0.86	Avg trade(win & loss)	$	638.67
Max consec. winners	13	Max consec. losers		3
Avg # bars in winners	20	Avg # bars in losers		12
Max intraday drawdown	$ -6500.00			
Profit factor	2.93	Max # contracts held		1
Account size required	$ 6500.00	Return on account		737%

— · — · — · — · — · — · — · — · — · — · — · — · — · — · —

Performance Summary: Long Trades

Total net profit	$ 40375.00	Open position P/L	$	0.00
Gross profit	$ 65225.00	Gross loss	$	-24850.00
Total # of trades	73	Percent profitable		77%
Number winning trades	56	Number losing trades		17
Largest winning trade	$ 6750.00	Largest losing trade	$	-2350.00
Average winning trade	$ 1164.73	Average losing trade	$	-1461.76
Ratio avg win/avg loss	0.80	Avg trade(win & loss)	$	553.08
Max consec. winners	13	Max consec. losers		3
Avg # bars in winners	19	Avg # bars in losers		12
Max intraday drawdown	$ -6500.00			
Profit factor	2.62	Max # contracts held		1
Account size required	$ 6500.00	Return on account		621%

— · — · — · — · — · — · — · — · — · — · — · — · — · — · —

Performance Summary: Short Trades

Total net profit	$ 7525.00	Open position P/L	$	0.00
Gross profit	$ 7525.00	Gross loss	$	0.00
Total # of trades	2	Percent profitable		100%
Number winning trades	2	Number losing trades		0
Largest winning trade	$ 7350.00	Largest losing trade	$	0.00
Average winning trade	$ 3762.50	Average losing trade	$	0.00
Ratio avg win/avg loss	100.00	Avg trade(win & loss)	$	3762.50
Max consec. winners	2	Max consec. losers		0
Avg # bars in winners	25	Avg # bars in losers		0
Max intraday drawdown	$ -1475.00			
Profit factor	100.00	Max # contracts held		1
Account size required	$ 1475.00	Return on account		510%

Figure 11-13. Historical record of the COR method holding positions beyond the day time frame.

ing the remaining unit in accordance with the parameters I have cited.

Summary

This chapter discussed the importance of closing versus opening relationships and presented the COR method for day trading. Specific rules of application were discussed. The assets and liabilities of the method were analyzed, along with specific historical test results. I also provided suggestions for maximizing results by holding positions for exit beyond the day time frame. Note that the COR method is a dynamic method that should be adjusted to market volatility and to individual markets.

12

Gap Methods
for Day Trading

*Take a straw and throw it up into the air, you
shall see by that which way the wind is.*
JOHN SELDEN

One of the more effective and specific methods of day trading is to
use an opening price gap as the first indication of a possible trade.
The basic method for trading, based on opening price gaps, has
already been discussed in detail in my book *The Compleat Day
Trader.* My discussion in this chapter will briefly review the basic
gap method and will give you an additional gap method that is a
variation on the theme.

A Day Trader's Dream

My years as a trader and market analyst have convinced me that
the more input a trader has in the formation of a trading decision,
the more likely that the decision will be wrong. While this may
not sound right, the fact is that it *is* right. Traders cannot help but
have their wishes, emotions, expectations, fears, and dreams inter-

fere with their decisions. Hence, the more a trader thinks about a trade—the more a trader analyzes a trade—the greater the probability that the trade will be a loser. I do not mean to denigrate the importance of the trader, yet facts are facts.

Unless you're an exceptional trader, you'll find that the more you spend in thought, the less you reap in profits. Traders don't need complicated systems; they need simple systems that don't require a great deal of judgment or thought. This is especially true of day-trading methods.

Some day traders are addicted to their quote screens, watching every tick as if their lives depended on it. And unfortunately it often does! My point of view is that if you want to sit and watch every price tick, you ought to just buy or lease an exchange membership and trade from the floor.

I believe that day trading should be a simple proposition, reasonably mechanical, and as objective as possible. Hence, the gap trade and its variation (to be discussed in this chapter) is the day trader's dream.

Oops!

The *gap trade* is a method that fits all of the important requirements of a day trader. I was originally introduced to the gap trade by Larry Williams, who deserves all of the credit for it. (Larry called it the *"oops"* signal for reasons that I'll explain later.)

The rules of application are simple. But before detailing them I'll define what I mean by a *gap*. In this case we are dealing with an *opening gap*, which is the first condition for entering a gap trade.

1. *Opening gap higher* (gap up). This occurs when the opening price for the day is higher than the high of the previous day. See Figure 12-1 for an ideal representation of the *gap higher* open. See Figure 12-2 for examples of gap higher openings. Note that when I refer to the "opening," I mean the first "print" price or the officially defined opening as determined by the given exchange.

2. *Opening gap lower* (*gap down*). This occurs when the opening price for the day is lower than the low of the previous day. See Figures 12-3 and 12-4. Again, by the "opening" I mean the first

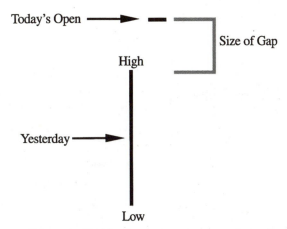

Figure 12-1. Ideal representation of a gap higher opening.

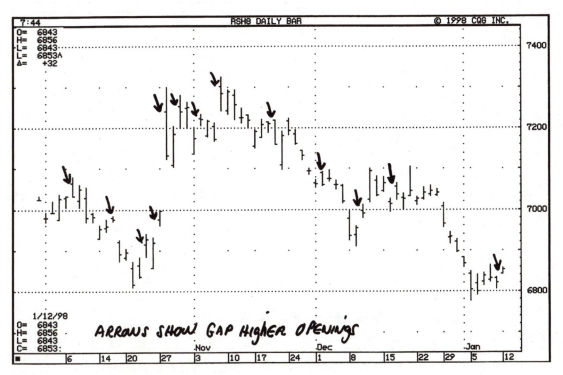

Figure 12-2. A daily chart of Swiss franc futures showing only gap higher openings.

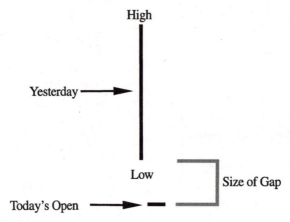

Figure 12-3. Ideal representation of a gap
lower opening.

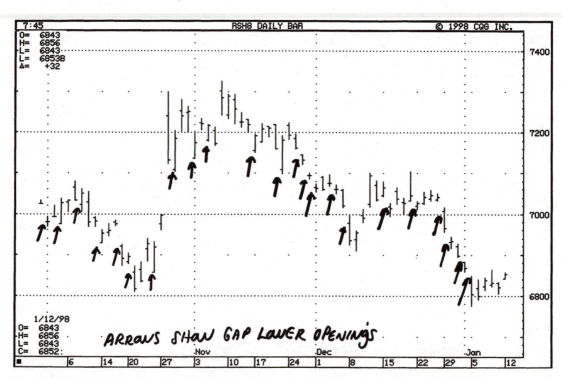

Figure 12-4. A daily chart of Swiss franc futures showing only gap lower openings.

"print" price or the officially defined opening as determined by the given exchange.

The opening gap *up* sets the precondition for a *short sale*. The opening gap *down* sets the precondition for a buy. Note that a gap up opening does not immediately give a sell short signal. It merely sets the first condition for a sell signal. A gap down opening does not immediately signal a buy. It merely sets the first condition for a buy signal.

How a Basic Gap Buy Signal Is Established

A basic gap buy signal occurs when a market opens on a *gap down* and then comes back up to penetrate the previous day's low by a given number of price ticks. When this occurs you *buy* for a day trade. You exit your trade either at a fixed-dollar-amount stop loss, a stop loss below the low of the day when you are filled, or MOC (market on close).

How a Basic Gap Sell Signal Is Established

A basic gap sell signal occurs when a market opens on a *gap up* and then comes back down to penetrate the previous day's high by a given number of price ticks. When this occurs, you *sell short* for a day trade. You exit your trade either at a fixed-dollar-amount stop loss, a stop loss above the high of the day when you are filled, or MOC (market on close).

As you can see, the rules of application for the gap trade are very simple. And the application of this methodology is simple as well. Figures 12-5 and 12-6 show ideal buy and sell signals. Figures 12-7 and 12-8 show actual buy and sell signals.

It should be noted that in trading gaps use only the *day session* prices. I repeat: In determining whether a gap has been made or not, do not use the overnight or Globex data. Gaps are determined based on day session data only! This is very important.

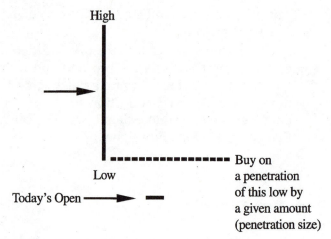

High

Low

Buy on
a penetration
of this low by
a given amount
(penetration size)

Today's Open ⟶ ▬

Figure 12-5. Ideal gap buy signal.

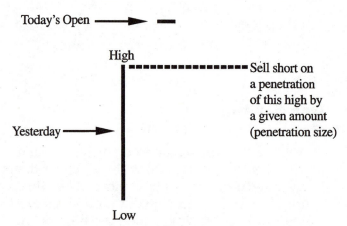

Today's Open ⟶ ▬

High

Sell short on
a penetration
of this high by
a given amount
(penetration size)

Yesterday ⟶

Low

Figure 12-6. Ideal gap sell signal.

Psychology of the Gap Trade

In the psychology of the gap trade is found the reason for its excellent ability to capture winning day trades. When a market opens on a down gap, traders often panic and sell out. If the market can absorb their selling and then move up high enough to penetrate the previous day's low, the sellers realize that they've made a mistake (*oops*, we've made a mistake) and enter their

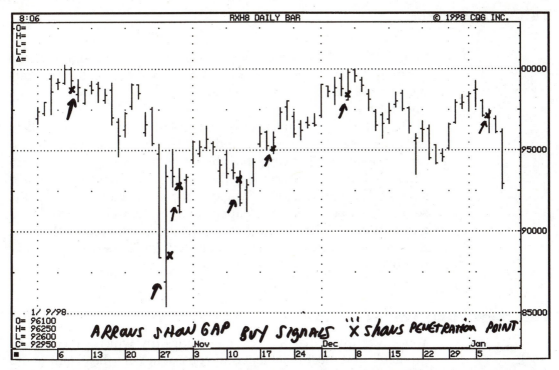

Figure 12-7. Actual gap buy signals. Arrows show gap buy signals; "X" shows penetration point.

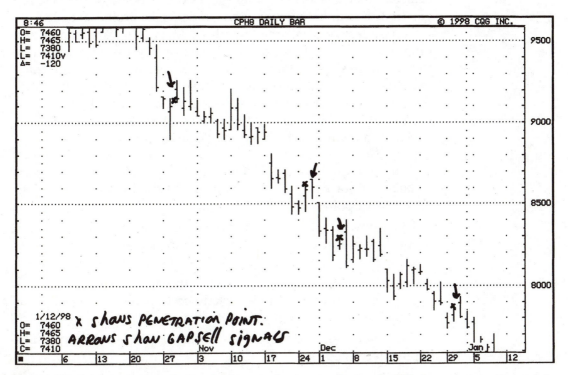

Figure 12-8. Actual gap sell signals. Arrows show gap sell signals; "X" shows penetration point.

longs again. At the same time, buyers waiting for a sign that the opening down gap was a bogus sign of weakness enter the market and bid prices higher. The market then usually closes near its high for the day.

The psychology of the sell gap is similar, only in reverse. Sellers exit en masse to cover shorts and to buy into new longs on a gap higher opening, thinking that the gap up is a sign of strength. When it fails to materialize, they exit and push prices down sharply. The psychology of the gap trade is, therefore, one of panic selling and panic buying. Gaps are highly correlated with tops and bottoms to the extent that gap trades occur frequently at or near market bottoms, whereas sell gap trades occur at or near market tops.

The "Best" Gap Trades

You might think that the best gap trades (by which I mean most profitable and most reliable) occur consistent with the extant trend. This is not necessarily true. Some of the best buy gap trades occur in bear markets as short covering panics occur. Some of the best sell gap trades occur in bull markets as traders take profits en masse.

Gap trades have had a noteworthy history. They are reliable and often profitable because they're based on the essential principle that underpins all trading psychology. As long as traders trade markets and as long as traders are human, gap trades will continue to work. And if they stop working, then I'm certain other psychologically based trading patterns will take their place.

Here is a review of the basic gap trade rules:

- To trade gaps the market must open either above the previous daily high or below the previous daily low by a given number of ticks or points.

- A gap buy signal is generated once the market has opened on a gap lower and then comes back up to penetrate the previous daily low by a given number of ticks.

- A gap sell signal is generated once the market has opened on a gap higher and then comes back down to penetrate the previous daily high by a given number of ticks.

- Gap buy or sell trades are closed out at the end of the day or at a predetermined stop loss.

Pragmatic Considerations
in Trading Gaps

While theory is one thing, reality is another. The reality of gap trading is that it is not appropriate in all markets and it is not appropriate at all times. The fact is that the two most important day-trading criteria must be met if the gap is to be used effectively: volume and volatility. Gap trades based on my rules can work well in markets such as S&P 500 futures, but they are doomed to failure in a market like oats, where trading volume is thin and where volatility is minimal (most of the time).

Another practical consideration is the use of stop losses. As you well know, there are three schools of thought on stop losses:

1. The best stop loss to use in a market is a risk management stop. In other words, risk a certain amount of money on each trade, and if the stop is hit, then exit.
2. A stop loss should be determined on the basis of your system and not on the basis of dollar risk.
3. A trailing stop loss should be used once a given profit target has been hit in order to preserve the profit.

These, then, are the basic stop loss strategies. Naturally, there are variations on the theme; however, my research has clearly indicated the following best strategies for gap trades as well as for most day trades.

- A dollar risk management stop loss is best as an initial stop.
- Once a given profit level has been achieved, a trailing stop loss is effective.
- The trailing stop loss must be a large one. In other words, you must be willing to risk up to 90 percent of your open profit, or you will be stopped out repeatedly.
- Small stop losses will work against you in gap trades, and in fact, a small stop loss will work against you in virtually all types of trading other than "scalping."

In some cases, holding a gap trade overnight may prove more profitable than exiting at the end of the trading session. But note that the trade would then no longer be considered a day trade. This method will be discussed later in this chapter.

Variations on the Gap Trade Theme

While the gap trade method is a viable method for day trading in active and volatile markets, I have discovered and researched several variations on the gap trade methodology that can make a significant difference in the bottom-line results. They are discussed below.

Gap Size. The size of the opening gap is important. Larry Williams, my colleague, friend of many years, and originator of the gap trade method, has often quipped "the bigger the gap, the better the trade," and I certainly agree with him. Shown in Figure 12-9 is a comparison of gap size and average profit per trade for gap trades in S&P futures covering the period from April 1982 (the inception of futures trading) through January 1998. I'm certain you'll agree that this is a sufficiently lengthy test period in terms of statistical validation.

The gap size figures suggest, but do not conclusively confirm, that a larger gap size is preferable. They do, however, show that there is a tendency for higher opening gap sizes to produce a larger average profit per trade than smaller gap sizes. A more effective approach is to use a different-size opening gap for buy signals and for sell signals. Since markets are not linear, this makes a great deal of sense. By varying the parameters, you will be able to fine-tune the gap trade method for a variety of markets.

Gap Penetration Size. This variable is also important. It measures how much the market penetrates back into its previous daily range for buy and sell signals. In other words, a smaller penetra-

Gap size (ticks)	Average trade ($)
2	173
3	125
5	50
10	316
15	296
35	377

Figure 12-9. Average profit per trade as a function of opening gap size in S&P gap trades 1982–1998. Longs and shorts.

Gap size	Average trade ($)	Percentage accuracy
2	120	56
5	189	58
10	393	60
15	425	61

Figure 12-10. Average profit per trade as a function of penetration size in S&P gap trades 1982–1998. Longs and shorts.

Stop loss ($)	Average trade ($)	Percentage accuracy
1000	512	58
1300	586	60
2000	550	60
2500	506	60
5000	556	62

Figure 12-11. Average profit per trade as a function of stop loss size in S&P gap trades 1982–1998. Longs and shorts.

tion size will give more trades. However, is it possible that a larger penetration size will give fewer trades but with higher accuracy? Figure 12-10 gives us an idea of how penetration size is related to average profit per trade.

The optimum numbers for gap penetration size were 10 ticks for longs and 12 ticks for shorts. The results using these entry gap sizes were 62 percent and $455 average trade for the period from 1982 through 1998 in S&P futures.

Stop Loss Size. Stop loss size is also very important. Shown in Figure 12-11 is a tabular listing of stop loss size with average profit per trade in S&P futures. As you can see, a larger stop loss is preferable for higher accuracy.

Period of Gap Comparison—
Multiple-Day Gap Signals

I am about to make a major change in the gap concept as presented heretofore, so hold on to your hat, since you'll need to have your thinking cap on for this one. While we know that the gap trade as I've discussed it so far is a good method for day trading, there is a variation on the theme of the gap trade that you may wish to consider. Consider the fact that a gap can be referenced back to the previous day or to any number of days back.

The Multiple-Day Gap Signal (Multigap)

The traditional or basic buy/sell gap signal has already been discussed in this chapter. The gap approach has merit; however, there is a variation on the theme of the gap trade method that may prove even more valuable. While the basic gap method is designed for day trading, there is a way to capitalize on the gap idea for short-term trades. The multigap is also useful for day trading, particularly in S&P futures where the accuracy and average trade increase. (I will show these statistics later after I explain the multigap method in detail.)

As you know, the basic gap signal occurs when a market opens below the low of its previous day and then penetrates the low on the way back up (buy signal) or when a market opens above the high of its previous day and then penetrates the high on the way back down. Entry is made on a buy or sell stop and exit is on the close of trading. In active markets such as S&P futures, this methodology has merit and back-tests profitably over many years of historical data. My recent test of the gap day trading method in S&P futures back to 1982 shows the system as having been correct 60 percent of the time with an average profit per trade of $497. This is very respectable for a day-trading method. There are ways to boost this figure to over 80 percent with nearly twice the average trade.

The Multigap Explained

The multigap is a simple method. Rather than generate a signal based on an opening gap above or below the previous day's high or low, the signal is generated based on an opening gap above or below the highest high or the lowest low of the last x number of days. The x is determined for each market based on the volatility characteristics of the market. What will work for S&P because of its volatility will not necessarily work for oats. Ideal examples of the multigap buy and sell signals are shown, respectively, in Figures 12-12 and 12-13.

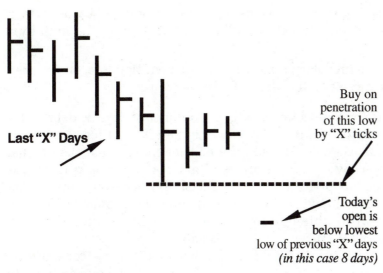

**Buy on
penetration
of this low
by "X" ticks**

Last "X" Days

Today's
open is
below lowest
low of previous "X" days
(in this case 8 days)

Figure 12-12. Multigap buy signal.

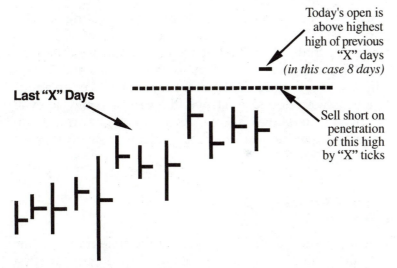

Today's open is
above highest
high of previous
"X" days
(in this case 8 days)

Last "X" Days

Sell short on
penetration
of this high
by "X" ticks

Figure 12-13. Multigap sell signal.

Rules of the Multigap Method

Following are some rules to keep in mind when using the multi-gap method:

■ If a market opens below its lowest low of the last x days, then buy on a penetration back up through the low by x ticks.

- If a market opens above its highest high of the last x days, then sell short on a penetration back down through the high by x ticks.

- Exit on a predetermined risk management stop loss, on the close of the day, or on the nth profitable opening

Note that by x days I mean a given number of days as defined for the indicated market. The x days can be different for buy signals and for sell signals. The nth profitable opening is also determined by market. By a *profitable opening* I mean an opening price that is above the buy price or below the sell short price. You simply count the number of days in which the opening was profitable. Then on the nth profitable opening, you exit (unless you have been stopped out first). See Figures 12-14 and 12-15.

This is a truly simple approach that I believe has considerable merit for position traders. You might want to take some time to evaluate this method. (See Figures 12-16 through 12-18 for additional historical test results.)

As mentioned, based on my initial historical testing in S&P futures from 1982 through 1998, I show an accuracy of 60 percent with an average trade of $482 (slippage and commission deducted). The entry parameters are 9 days for buy signals and 2 days for sell signals. In order to find the best fit, you will need to adjust gap size and penetration size. Hence, the results could be even better than what is stated above. As you can see, this is an improvement on the basic gap method previously described. See Figures 12-16 and 12-17.

Holding beyond the Day Time Frame (Exit on *Nth Profitable Opening*)

Sometimes it pays to hold slightly beyond the time frame of one day. Using the multigap method in S&P and exiting on the first profitable opening, my initial historical testing in S&P futures from 1982 through 1998 shows an accuracy of 85 percent with an average trade of $780 (slippage and commissions deducted) based on a window of 9 days for buy signals, 2 days for sell signals, and a few more parameters for stop-loss and amount of gap penetration. See Figure 12-18.

In some markets, gap trades that show a poor record of success when closed out at the end of the day can improve dramatically

Figure 12-14. Multiple-day gap trades in S&P 500.

```
jb.Gap System  S&P 500 INDEX 55/99-Daily   04/21/82 - 01/02/98

                 Performance Summary:  All Trades

Total net profit      $  85350.00  Open position P/L    $       0.00
Gross profit          $ 155700.00  Gross loss           $  -70350.00

Total # of trades          177     Percent profitable        60%
Number winning trades      107     Number losing trades       70

Largest winning trade $  25125.00  Largest losing trade $   -4575.00
Average winning trade $   1455.14  Average losing trade $   -1005.00
Ratio avg win/avg loss      1.45   Avg trade(win & loss)$     482.20

Max consec. winners          9     Max consec. losers          4
Avg # bars in winners        0     Avg # bars in losers        0

Max intraday drawdown $ -10700.00
Profit factor               2.21   Max # contracts held        1
Account size required $  10700.00  Return on account         798%
- - - - - - - - - - - - - - - - - - - - - - - - - - - - - - - - -

                 Performance Summary:  Long Trades

Total net profit      $  48025.00  Open position P/L    $       0.00
Gross profit          $  71050.00  Gross loss           $  -23025.00

Total # of trades           50     Percent profitable        68%
Number winning trades       34     Number losing trades       16

Largest winning trade $  25125.00  Largest losing trade $   -4575.00
Average winning trade $   2089.71  Average losing trade $   -1439.06
Ratio avg win/avg loss      1.45   Avg trade(win & loss)$     960.50

Max consec. winners          8     Max consec. losers          4
Avg # bars in winners        0     Avg # bars in losers        0

Max intraday drawdown $  -9925.00
Profit factor               3.09   Max # contracts held        1
Account size required $   9925.00  Return on account         484%
- - - - - - - - - - - - - - - - - - - - - - - - - - - - - - - - -

                 Performance Summary:  Short Trades

Total net profit      $  37325.00  Open position P/L    $       0.00
Gross profit          $  84650.00  Gross loss           $  -47325.00

Total # of trades          127     Percent profitable        57%
Number winning trades       73     Number losing trades       54

Largest winning trade $   6850.00  Largest losing trade $   -4575.00
Average winning trade $   1159.59  Average losing trade $    -876.39
Ratio avg win/avg loss      1.32   Avg trade(win & loss)$     293.90

Max consec. winners          8     Max consec. losers          5
Avg # bars in winners        0     Avg # bars in losers        0

Max intraday drawdown $  -9825.00
Profit factor               1.79   Max # contracts held        1
Account size required $   9825.00  Return on account         380%
```

Figure 12-15. Historical record of multiple-day gap trade S&P 500 1982–1998.

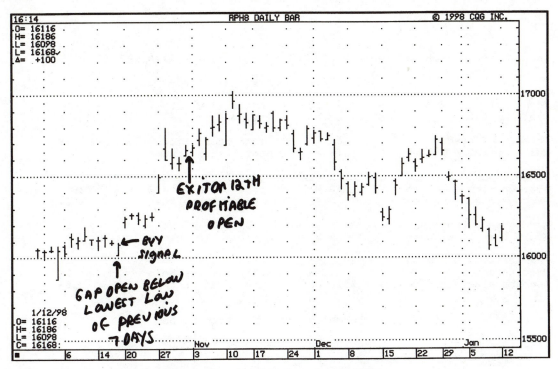

Figure 12-16. Multigap buy signal and exit in British pound futures.

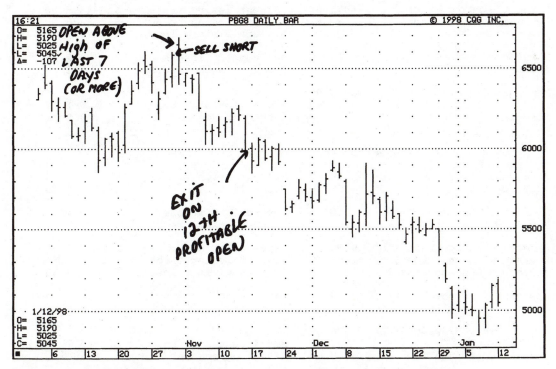

Figure 12-17. Multigap sell signal and exit in pork belly futures.

```
jb.Gap System  S&P 500 INDEX 55/99-Daily   04/21/82 - 01/02/98
```

Performance Summary: All Trades

Total net profit	$ 131875.00	Open position P/L	$ 0.00
Gross profit	$ 220250.00	Gross loss	$ -88375.00
Total # of trades	169	Percent profitable	85%
Number winning trades	143	Number losing trades	26
Largest winning trade	$ 26875.00	Largest losing trade	$ -5600.00
Average winning trade	$ 1540.21	Average losing trade	$ -3399.04
Ratio avg win/avg loss	0.45	Avg trade(win & loss)	$ 780.33
Max consec. winners	18	Max consec. losers	2
Avg # bars in winners	2	Avg # bars in losers	3
Max intraday drawdown	$ -12850.00		
Profit factor	2.49	Max # contracts held	1
Account size required	$ 12850.00	Return on account	1026%

Performance Summary: Long Trades

Total net profit	$ 66175.00	Open position P/L	$ 0.00
Gross profit	$ 89100.00	Gross loss	$ -22925.00
Total # of trades	49	Percent profitable	86%
Number winning trades	42	Number losing trades	7
Largest winning trade	$ 26875.00	Largest losing trade	$ -4575.00
Average winning trade	$ 2121.43	Average losing trade	$ -3275.00
Ratio avg win/avg loss	0.65	Avg trade(win & loss)	$ 1350.51
Max consec. winners	14	Max consec. losers	2
Avg # bars in winners	1	Avg # bars in losers	1
Max intraday drawdown	$ -8050.00		
Profit factor	3.89	Max # contracts held	1
Account size required	$ 8050.00	Return on account	822%

Performance Summary: Short Trades

Total net profit	$ 65700.00	Open position P/L	$ 0.00
Gross profit	$ 131150.00	Gross loss	$ -65450.00
Total # of trades	120	Percent profitable	84%
Number winning trades	101	Number losing trades	19
Largest winning trade	$ 9050.00	Largest losing trade	$ -5600.00
Average winning trade	$ 1298.51	Average losing trade	$ -3444.74
Ratio avg win/avg loss	0.38	Avg trade(win & loss)	$ 547.50
Max consec. winners	19	Max consec. losers	2
Avg # bars in winners	2	Avg # bars in losers	4
Max intraday drawdown	$ -13575.00		
Profit factor	2.00	Max # contracts held	1
Account size required	$ 13575.00	Return on account	484%

Figure 12-18. Multiple-day S&P 500 gap trades with exit on first profitable opening using parameters.

using the multigap method. In T-bond futures, for example, the simple gap method back-test in T-bonds shows a 50 percent accuracy with an average trade of only $56. But holding the trade with an exit on the first profitable opening yields an 85 percent with an average trade of over $224 for the period from 1978 to 1998.

As another example, the basic gap trade in coffee futures produces an average trade of $137 with 54 percent accuracy if exited on the close. However, using the multigap method, accuracy increases to 67 percent with an average trade of $424 over the period from August 1973 through January 1998.

Take a little time to review this approach in a number of different markets. You may find it worth your while to pursue it.

Intraday Follow-Up of Gap Trades

Finally, another aspect of the gap trade is the trailing stop loss. For those who are active day traders, a trailing stop loss method may be a valuable addition to the gap trade and/or the multigap trade. Use the guidelines presented previously in this book to implement a trailing stop loss.

Summary

The basic gap trade as I have previously presented it in *The Compleat Day Trader* and in this chapter is a basically sound method. It performs best in S&P futures. A variation on the basic gap method is the multigap method. The motivated trader will take a little time and effort to find the best combination of the major variables associated with both the gap trade and the multigap trade. These variables are length of days in gap window, the size of the gap, the size of the gap penetration, and the stop loss. Another effective method would be to use a trailing stop loss once a gap trade or multigap trade has been entered. While the trailing stop loss may decrease accuracy slightly in some cases, there are markets in which accuracy increases, as well as average profit per trade.

13

Accumulation Distribution Oscillator Derivative

Fortid fortuna adiuvat.
Fortune favors the brave.   Terence

For many years traders have attempted to find a method that will give insight as to the locus of control in a market. By this I mean the balance of power. The question as to whether the bulls or the bears are "in control" of a market is an important one, particularly for the day trader. If we know that the bulls are in control of a market, then we will do well to buy on declines, knowing that the market is likely to recover quickly from its drop. In a market that is controlled by the bears, rallies will be relatively short-lived, as sellers overpower buyers and the market returns to its declining trend.

By "control" I do not mean to imply that there is an actual group of buyers or sellers who are conspiring to control the direction of a market. Rather, I mean essentially "balance of power." In effect, the amount of buying power exceeds the amount of selling power or vice versa. Certainly, the balance of power will shift at some point, usually after the buying power and the selling pressure have reached a point of equilibrium and the tide changes direction. Although the trend can change rapidly in some instances, there are usually warning signs that precede changes in trend.

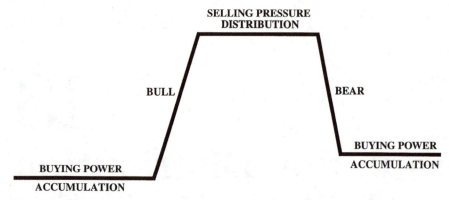

Figure 13-1. Ideal representation of buying power versus selling pressure.

At times the indications are subtle, and at times they are obvious. But this is not always the case. And this is what makes trading systems imperfect. There is no certain way I know to detect when the balance of power will shift. The ideal situation of buying power versus selling pressure can be depicted graphically as shown in Figure 13-1.

The Ideal Situation

In a perfect world we would like to see markets follow our paradigm as closely as possible. While this would make our task as traders more definitive, it would likely mean an end to free markets, since virtually every market trend and trend change would be predictable and there would, therefore, be no need to trade. Figure 13-1 illustrates the phases of a "normal" market as it moves from a neutral phase to a bullish phase and then to topping, bearish, and bottoming phases.

The accompanying 10-minute Swiss franc futures chart (Figure 13-2) shows how a market enters a topping time frame and then turns lower. Theoretically, as the market moves sideways, a change of control is taking place as the bears gain the upper hand. One interpretation of what is actually happening is that selling pressure outweighs buying power. During this sideways phase the bears are "distributing" contracts to the bulls. The bulls eventually reach a point where their cumulative buying can no longer sustain an uptrend, and the market drops as the bears continue their cumulative selling.

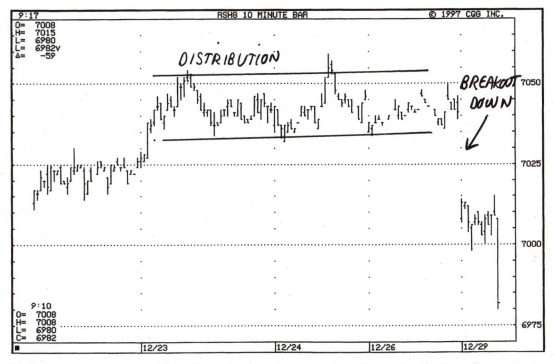

Figure 13-2. 10-minute Swiss franc futures showing a topping or distribution phase prior to a decline.

At a market bottom the reverse holds true. In theory, the buying power outweighs the selling pressure. There is cumulatively more buying than there is selling. Eventually the balance is overcome as buying demand outpaces the supply of selling, and the market surges higher as the bulls gain firm control of the market. Figure 13-3 shows an accumulation pattern in the 10-minute S&P 500 futures chart. Note that the market enters a period of sideways movement prior to a sharp rally. Theoretically, the bulls are slowly but surely gaining control of the market during the bottoming or "accumulation" phase.

Note that the situation I have described herein is an ideal situation. Markets do not always follow their ideal situations. At times a market will change trend almost immediately and seemingly without notice. Purists will argue that in such cases markets do give advance warnings but that the signs are subtle. I do not disagree. However, I note that if the signs cannot be found, then the theory, no matter how cogent and valid, will not help us.

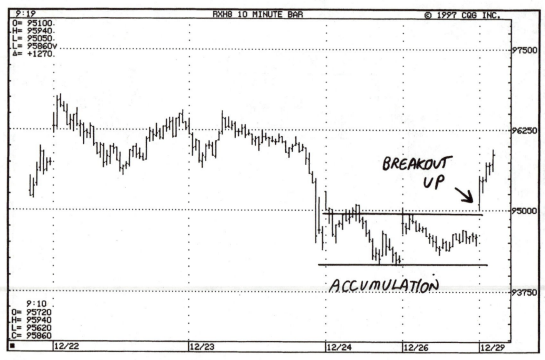

Figure 13-3. 10-minute S&P 500 futures showing a bottoming or accumulation phase prior to a rally.

Accumulation/Distribution Theory

What I have just described for you is the theory of accumulation and distribution. The theory has face validity and is certainly easy to understand. The difficult part is finding methods, indicators, and/or technical trading systems that will allow traders to take advantage of the hypothetical constructs. One such indicator is the advance/decline (A/D) oscillator originally developed by Larry Williams and James J. Waters in 1972. Their article entitled "Measuring Market Momentum" in the October 1972 issue of *Commodities Magazine* introduced their A/D oscillator.

The purpose of the oscillator was to detect changes in the balance of power from buyers to sellers and vice versa. Calculation of the A/D oscillator is a relatively simple matter. A thorough explanation and critical evaluation of the A/D oscillator can be found in *The New Commodity Trading Systems and Methods.** The A/D oscillator is also available in preprogrammed form on many of the popular software analysis systems such as CQG (Commodity Quote Graphics). The formula for calculating A/D can be obtained either in the original Williams and Waters article or the Kaufman book cited above.

Using the A/D Oscillator

There are several potential applications of the A/D oscillator for position and day trading. They range from the artistic and inter- pretive to the mechanical and objective. Since this book is not about art but about the quasi-science of technical analysis, I will refrain from a discussion of the artistic application of the A/D oscillator. While my application may not be as scientific as one would like, my efforts are in the correct direction. One method I have worked with extensively is to buy and sell based on A/D oscillator crosses above and below the zero line. The construc- tion of the oscillator suggests that when the A/D value is above zero, the market is under accumulation, or the bulls are in con- trol.

Conversely, when the A/D value is below zero the bears are in control of the market. Theoretically, when the A/D crosses from plus to minus, a market crosses from bullish to bearish and vice versa. Figures 13-4 through 13-6 support the argument, each showing the A/D oscillator and market trend. Note how the A/D oscillator has the uncanny ability to remain negative for a lengthy period of time as prices continue to decline or positive for a lengthy period of time as prices continue to rally. That's the good news about the A/D oscillator. The bad news is that these are ideal situations that do not occur as frequently as we would like. All too often markets move higher and higher while the A/D is in negative ground and vice versa. Such situations not only confuse the trader into thinking that the theory is incorrect, but they are also costly, since they produce losses. Yet another limitation of the A/D and, indeed, of all oscillators, is that they can frequently

*Perry Kaufman, *The New Commodity Trading Systems and Methods*, Wiley, New York, 1987, pp. 102–106.

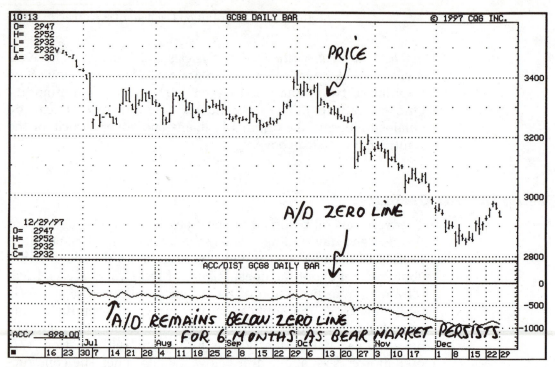

Figure 13-4. Daily February 1998 gold futures showing negative A/D reading for over 6 months of a bear trend.

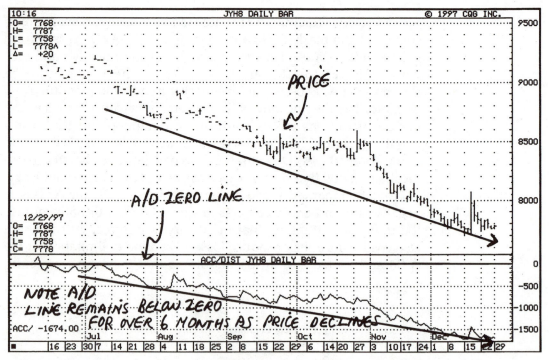

Figure 13-5. Daily March 1998 yen futures showing negative A/D reading for over 6 months of a bear trend.

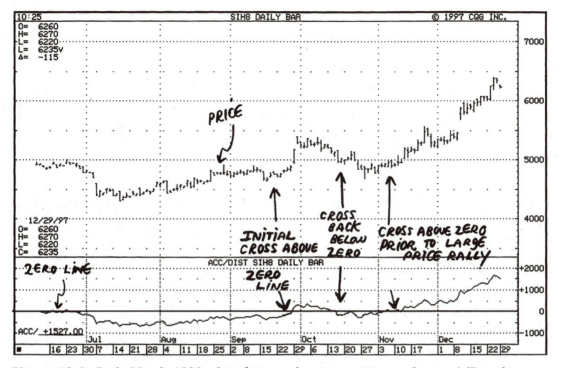

Figure 13-6. Daily March 1998 silver futures showing positive reading in A/D and a sustained bull trend.

move back and forth above and below the zero line numerous times before a sustained trend emerges. Traders who buy and sell on such frequent crosses above and below the zero line will suffer numerous repeated losses, not to mention the cost of commissions and slippage.

As an example, of this limitation, consider Figure 13-7. This figure shows March 1998 coffee futures with an A/D oscillator that remains negative until the top of the market in December 1997. After the oscillator crosses into positive ground, the market tops and declines sharply. How can such a severe limitation be overcome? The approach I suggest is to use a derivative of the A/D line that will generate signals when the A/D line crosses above and below its first derivative. In this case the derivative will be a moving average of the A/D line as explained in the next section.

Figure 13-7. The A/D oscillator crosses into positive ground at the top of a move after remaining negative throughout a large rally from the October/November lows.

The Advance/Decline Derivative (ADD)

The term *derivative* means exactly what it says. The first derivative of any value is a new value that is derived from the initial value. If, for example, I have a 24-day moving average as my original value, and then I calculate a 20-day moving average of the 24-day moving average, then the 20-day moving average is the first derivative of the 24-day moving average. If I calculate a moving average of the A/D oscillator, then the moving average I calculate is termed the first derivative of the A/D line, since it is derived from the A/D value. One purpose of calculating a derivative is to smooth the values of the original data. Our purpose is to do this as well as to use the derivative value and the A/D value in order to generate signals that will help overcome the limitations of the A/D oscillator when used alone (as cited earlier).

Beginning with the A/D values we will calculate a moving average of the A/D and plot both lines on the same chart against price. We will use the crossover points of the two values as our buy and sell points for day trading. As an example, consider Figure 13-8. It shows the A/D oscillator with a 28-period simple moving average of the A/D oscillator. I have marked the lines accordingly. The chart does not include the underlying market. It merely shows the two lines as well as the points at which they cross over one another. My method buys and sells when crossovers occur. But note that there are several additional rules for buying and selling on crossovers; these will be explained shortly. For the time being, please examine my notes in Figure 13-8. Now examine 13-9. It shows the same chart with the actual market prices above it. I have marked the crossover points on the A/D and price chart for illustration.

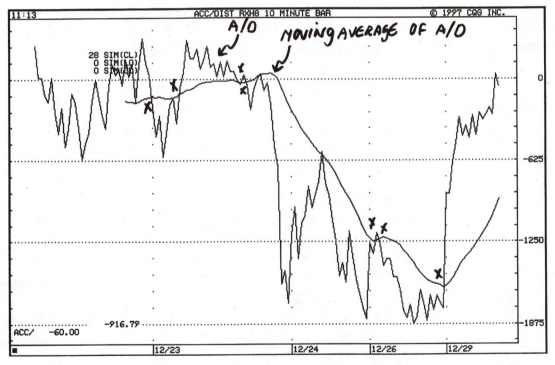

Figure 13-8. A/D Line and 28-period simple MA of A/D line. Note crossovers marked "X."

Figure 13-9. A/D oscillator and its moving average plotted against price.

ADD Signals

In order to use the ADD for day trading (or position trading), we must have a set of rules for entry and exit. These rules are as follows:

- Compute the A/D values.
- Compute a simple 28-period moving average of the A/D values.
- A *buy signal* occurs when the A/D line crosses *above* its moving average after being below it.
- A *sell signal* occurs when the A/D line crosses *below* its moving average after being above it.
- In order for a signal to be valid, the crossover must remain in effect for at least two postings of the values. This is done in order to avoid whipsaw moves.
- All trades are exited at the end of the day session—win, lose, or draw.

- New trades can be entered the next day either on the open based on the direction of the last signal or you can wait for a new signal.

Figures 13-10 through 13-15 illustrate the rules as applied above as well as the buy and sell points on intraday price charts.

Caveats and Considerations

As presented here, the ADD method is objective but not entirely systematic. In order to use it as a system, you will need to add a risk management stop loss and/or a trailing stop loss (if you prefer). This will make the method useful as a system. Naturally, you will want to trade the ADD in active and volatile markets only. The ADD method also has potential for use in day trading volatile spreads.

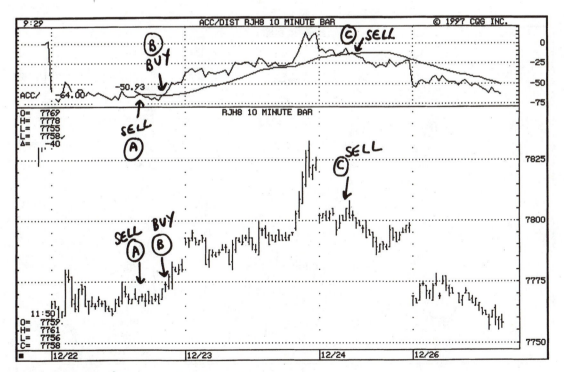

Figure 13-10. ADD buy and sell signals.

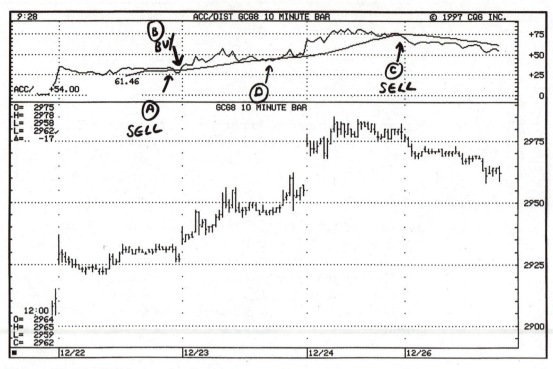

Figure 13-11. ADD buy and sell signals.

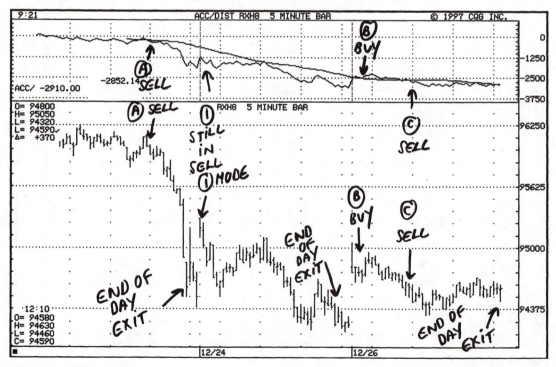

Figure 13-12. ADD buy and sell signals.

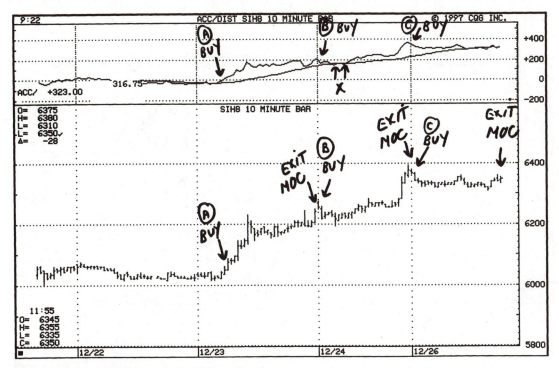

Figure 13-13. ADD buy and sell signals.

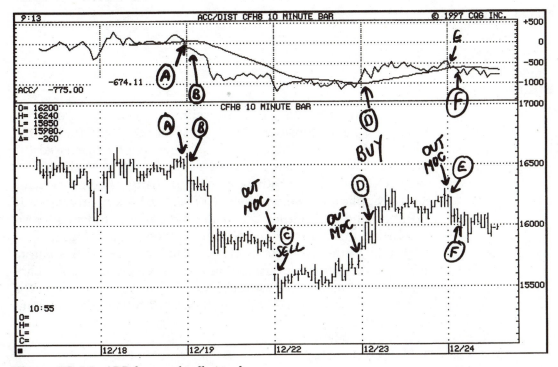

Figure 13-14. ADD buy and sell signals.

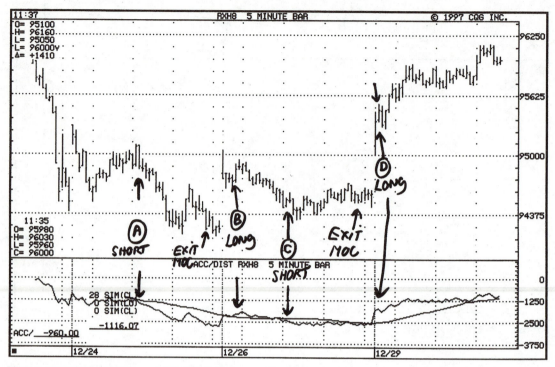

Figure 13-15. ADD buy and sell signals.

Summary

The accumulation/distribution oscillator (A/D) is a powerful oscillator that has considerable potential for use in day trading flat positions as well as volatile spreads. This chapter discussed the basic A/D oscillator and introduced the idea of the A/D derivative (ADD) as a timing indicator or trend change method. Specific rules of application were presented. The ADD is a highly versatile indicator lending itself for use in all time frames. Traders interested in using this approach are encouraged to research it more thoroughly as a trading system with risk management rules before using it extensively for day trading. As I have noted in this chapter, the ADD method is not offered as a system at this time. It is merely a method that could be systematized by adding risk management rules.

14

The Importance
of Orders

Praise the Lord and pass the ammunition.
LT. CMDR FORGY AT PEARL HARBOR

To the day trader (in fact to all traders), using the right price order is just as important as using the right tool is to the mechanic or carpenter. Using the right orders can spell the difference between profits and losses. Using a market order when a stop or stop limit order should have been used may result in a poor price fill that will cost you dollars. Since the bottom line is very important to day traders, perhaps more important than to any other type of trader other than a scalper (who is also a day trader), every tick saved is indeed a tick earned. Orders should be specifically geared to what you seek to achieve in terms of timing your trading system. Orders are designed to save you money, not to lose you money. They will help you reduce bad fills and avoid lost points or price skids. But to use price orders to your advantage, you must be familiar with the various types of orders and when they are best used. You must also know what orders to avoid and when to avoid them.

What You Should Know about Market Orders

Market orders must be avoided whenever possible. A market order is, as far as I'm concerned, a license to steal. Rarely will a market order be filled at the exact price you are expecting. Typically, a market order will cost you one tick, at times two or three. In S&P futures, a market order may cost you much more than just a few ticks, although one or two ticks in a quiet market is not unusual. If you lose two ticks on entry and two ticks on exit, the cost per trade will most assuredly add up. However, not using market orders will cause you to risk not getting a position at all or not being able to exit a position at all. Here are some guidelines for using market orders:

- *Only use a market order when absolutely necessary.* If you are using an intraday oscillator-type signal that enters at the end of a given time segment, then a market order is acceptable. If, however, you can use a specific price order as opposed to a market order, this is preferable. It is not uncommon for markets to make a quick move following a signal, but very often the market returns to its original entry price fairly soon, and a price order would have been sufficient. You can save a great deal of money this way.

- *If you are riding a fairly large profit* and wish to exit a position quickly because your indicators have turned, then it is worth giving some of the profit back just to make sure you are out of your position.

- *Avoid market-on-close (MOC) orders.* All too often such orders are even more of a license to steal, since they can be filled at almost any price during the last minute of trading. An MOC order in thin markets is a certain invitation to trouble. Many traders jokingly refer to MOCs as "murder-on-close" orders, since fills are often so poor.

- *Never use market orders with spreads.* You are far better off using specific spread levels for entry and exit, or you may use specific price orders in each market individually to "leg" into or out of the spread. Considerable slippage is the rule in spread market orders. Unfortunately, the only orders you can use in spreads are market orders or price orders. Of the two types, price orders are clearly preferable.

Market-If-Touched (MIT) Orders

An MIT order to buy is always placed below the market, and an MIT order to sell is placed above the market. An MIT order becomes a market order when hit. Therefore, if you have an MIT order to buy at 4150, this order will become a market order as soon as a trade occurs at 4150. The pit broker holding this order will immediately buy at the market. You could get filled at any price; however, you will usually be filled at or near your order, at times better than your price and at times worse. This is the chance you take when using such an order. An MIT order is used when you have a specific price level in mind for entry and you do not wish to take the chance of not being filled. Ordinarily such orders are used for selling at resistance above the market or for buying at support below the market.

The day trader who is using the support and resistance methods described in this book may use MIT orders; however, do note that such orders can cost you a few ticks. MITs are, however, excellent orders to use when trading support and resistance levels. Remember that such orders are not accepted by all exchanges nor are they accepted at all times. Under certain market conditions MIT orders may be refused at the discretion either of the pit broker or of the exchange.

Fill-or-Kill (FOK) Orders

A fill-or-kill order is given at a specific price with the understanding that the pit broker will attempt to fill your order three times in succession at the requested price. Hence, if you have an FOK order to sell at 4550, the broker who gets your order will offer at 4550 three times. If there is no fill, the broker will immediately cancel, or "kill," your order, and the kill will be reported back to you. The advantage of this order is that you will be able to place it at a specific price, and you will get very quick feedback as to whether it has been filled. And that's important!

Be aware, however, that not all exchanges or brokers accept FOK orders. Under certain market conditions such orders may be refused. Some brokers will become irritated if you use too many FOK orders that go unfilled, since it takes time and person power to place these orders. Discount brokers may be especially unhappy if you use too many FOK orders.

Finally, do not place your orders too far from the market, or they will not get filled. This will be even more aggravating for your broker. If you plan to use FOK orders, then please use orders that are very close to the current price. If you abuse these orders, you will frustrate your broker and you will lose the respect of the order takers.

FOK orders are useful in virtually all situations where entry at the market should be avoided but where there is a need to establish or liquidate a position. Remember that using an FOK order does not guarantee a price fill; it merely guarantees that you will be filled at your price or better or not at all.

Stop Orders

Stop orders are placed either above or below the market. These orders are especially good for exiting positions when they go against you or for entering markets on breakouts. The problem with stop orders is that you will not necessarily be filled at your price in a fast market. Frequently many sharp and sudden moves in the currencies, T-bond futures, or S&P futures will result in considerable slippage of buy-and-sell stop orders. The best way to avoid this is to use a stop limit order, described below.

Stop Limit Orders

A stop limit order is a stop order with a price limit on it. The reason for using such an order is to allow more flexibility in obtaining a fill. Therefore, when you place a buy stop limit order at 6450 with a limit of 6465, this means that you will accept a fill within these limits inclusive. The good part of such an order is that it permits the floor broker more leeway in filling you and therefore improves the odds that you will be filled. Such an order protects you from too much slippage. Stop limit orders should be used more often, although few traders actually use them.

Good-Till-Canceled Orders

A good-till-canceled order does exactly what its name suggests. It is an order that will remain in the market until canceled or filled. This order is also called an *open order*. Typically all open orders are canceled by your broker at the end of each calendar month and must be reinstated. In practice, day traders have no need for GTC or open orders, since their work is done at the end of each day.

One Cancels the Other (OCO)

This is an order qualifier. It allows a trader to have two orders entered simultaneously with the cancellation of one contingent upon the fulfillment of the other. In other words, when one of the orders is filled, the other will be canceled. This is a good way of bracketing markets for either of two possible outcomes. As in the case of several other orders noted previously, some exchanges do not accept such orders.

Using Orders to Your Advantage

Now that you've read about the different types of orders, here are some suggestions regarding their use. The purpose of learning how to use price orders to your advantage is obvious. Profitable day trading depends on making every penny and every point count. You must be consistent and frugal in everything you do. Here is a list of dos and don'ts with respect to orders:

- *Try to avoid using market orders unless absolutely necessary.* Market orders cost you ticks. If you lose a few ticks getting in and a few ticks getting out, then you have lost good money, often unnecessarily. There are many good alternatives to market orders. Some of them have been discussed previously; others will be discussed later.

- *Don't use MOC orders.* They will cost you ticks, and ticks add up. A few ticks here, a few ticks there—pretty soon it adds up to real money. If you must use such an order, then you are probably better off selling at the market several minutes before the close than in giving your broker an MOC order. Again, as far as I'm concerned an MOC is, most often, a license to steal.

- *Use stop limit orders instead of stop orders.* In most cases you will be filled. If you are concerned about being filled, put a one- or two-tick limit on your order.

- *Fill-or-kill orders can be used to your advantage in several ways.* If you need to exit or enter a trade and you don't want to wait to find out if you've been filled, then use an FOK order. You'll get quick feedback, and you'll probably save money. If you've never used such orders before, then get your feet wet.

- *Use FOK orders to test a market.* One good way to see how strong or weak a market may be is to use an FOK order. Here's what I mean: Let's say that June S&P futures are trading between 406.50 and 406.90. You had a buy signal at 406.50. Trading volume is light. Following the buy signal, prices moved quickly to 406.90, and you didn't want to chase the market. You are concerned that the signal might not work this time, because the market fell back quickly to the original breakout price of 406.50. You are therefore hesitant to buy. What to do?

  Test the market by placing an FOK order to go long at 406.45 or 406.40, knowing that this is below the recent range of trades. Your order goes in and you watch the tape. It reads 406.55 when you enter your order. The ticks then go as follows: 406.55 . . . 406.50 . . . 406.53 . . . 406.50 . . . 406.50 . . . 406.45B (your bid) . . . 406.45. You are filled at your bid price. What does this mean about the character of the market? Most likely this indicates a market that is weak. You were filled at a low bid, and this means that there are willing sellers. This characterizes a weak market.

  However, consider the same scenario with a different outcome. You enter your bid at 406.45 FOK. The tape reads 406.55 when you enter your order. The ticks then go as follows: 406.55 . . . 406.50 . . . 406.55 . . . 406.50 . . . 406.50 . . . 406.55 . . . 436.55 . . . 406.60 . . . 406.65 . . . 406.60 . . . 406.55 . . . 406.60 . . . 406.65 . . . 406.70 . . . 406.75 . . . and so on. The market never even comes close to your bid, and the order is returned killed. What does this mean? It indicates a market with good demand. It suggests that you had better get on board quickly. You may even want to use a market order to do so.

- *MIT orders are acceptable but not always efficient.* They are good for trading within a support/resistance channel, but they will cost you ticks.

- *OCO orders, where accepted, are very helpful.* They will help you bracket the market with different strategies and should be used wherever needed.

- *Specify first open only.* Some New York markets have staggered openings. In these markets each contract month is opened individually in chronological order, traded for a few minutes, and then closed so that another month may be opened. Once the process has been completed, all months are opened again at the same time. The same procedure is used for closing. Should you need to get into one of these markets on the open, specify that you want your order good for the first open only. All too often the second opening price is distinctly different from the first open. This can cost you money.

- *Insist on prompt reporting of order fills.* It is absolutely necessary for you to know when you've been filled and when you've not been filled. You must be strict with your broker in demanding fills back as soon as possible. Do not accept excuses, particularly in currencies, T-bonds, S&P futures, and petroleum futures, where *flash fills* are easily given. A flash fill is one for which you may remain on hold as your order is hand-signaled to the pit. Although there will be some conditions in which delays are understandable, such delays are anathema to the day trader and must be avoided whenever and wherever possible.

- *Know which exchanges will accept certain orders.* The rules change from time to time and from one market condition to another. If you don't know the rules, find them out. The Chicago Mercantile and IMM will accept almost all orders almost all the time. The Chicago Board of Trade is a stickler for accepting only certain types of orders—it does not accept MITs. Some New York markets have restrictions as well. Orange juice is one of the most notorious markets, but then you probably don't want to and shouldn't day trade OJ.

- *Find out how your broker places your orders.* Does he or she call the floor? Are your orders put on a wire for execution? Does your broker need to call someone, who will call someone else, who will then call someone else? This all takes time. Day traders can't afford the time for such delays. Ask your broker for his or her procedures and deal only with those brokers who can get you the fastest fills. Anything else will cost you money no matter how low the commission rate. Don't be penny-wise and pound-foolish.

- *Globex (24-hour) trading requires even more discretion in order placement.* Be very careful. Learn the rules and learn to deal with the lack of liquidity.

- *If trading futures options, use price orders all the time.* A market order in options will frequently bring you shockingly bad results due to the poor liquidity. *Always* use price orders in futures options!

- *Learn how to place orders.* Make sure your terminology is correct, make certain you mean what you say, and make sure you listen to the order as it is repeated back to you. You are liable for your orders. Errors will cost you.

- Don't beat around the bush. When you place your orders, speak quickly, decisively, and clearly.

- *Keep a written record of your orders.* Even if you trade only one market, once a day, keep a written record that includes the market, whether you bought or sold, the type of order, the quantity, the price at which you were filled, your order number (as given to you by the order taker), and the time you placed the order. Don't fail to note all the above. It will save you a great deal of money in the long run.

- *Report all errors immediately.* The longer you wait to report an error, the smaller the odds of having it rectified.

- *Always check out at the end of the day, especially if you have traded a great deal.* By *check out* I mean make certain you have received all your fills and that you have closed out all your trades. Many brokerage firms will send you a preliminary run at the end of the day via modem. Print out the run and check it against your order sheet. Report all errors immediately!

- Check your order sheet before market closing to make certain you have taken the necessary steps to close out positions. The more you trade and the larger your positions, the more important this will be.

These are just a few suggestions that will help you master the pragmatic end-of-day trading. Don't ever discount the importance of proper order placement and consistent procedures. The wrong order in the wrong market can cost you plenty. I know. I've made all these mistakes at one time or another, and I don't want you to have to repeat them. Learn it from me the easy way—don't learn it the hard way by losing money.

Summary

Too many traders are either ignorant of, or uninformed about, the importance of orders. The day trader must make the most of each trade. Therefore, saving a tick here and a tick there can eventually add up to a considerable sum of money. Although the day trader will most often use market orders, there are numerous situations in which other types of orders are either preferable or dictated by the nature of the system that is being used. This chapter defined the various types of orders, indicating when they are best used and under what conditions certain orders might be better or worse than others.

15

The Psychology
of Day Trading

He bears the seed of ruin in himself.
MATTHEW ARNOLD

Day trading is, at the same time, less psychologically demanding and more psychologically demanding than position trading. On the one hand, day trading requires more discipline and self-control than does position trading; on the other hand, there is a certain peace of mind that comes with the knowledge that you are "clean and clear" at the end of the day. When people have asked me why I prefer day trading to position trading, I quickly reply that "I like to sleep at night." While this may seem at first blush to be a flippant response, there is much truth to it. The good news about day trading is that it permits the trader to walk away from the markets at day's end knowing that there is nothing that can happen overnight to affect his or her account balance other than a total economic collapse or bankruptcy of the firm that carries the account.

Position traders, however, will argue that by limiting one's trading to the time frame of 1 day, potentially significant profit opportunities are lost. And this may very well be the case. But trading opportunities are very much like paying taxes—it's not what you make, it's what you keep that's important. Note also that there is nothing to prevent a day trader from being a position trader as well (although I advise you to separate these methods of trading by having a different account for each). In the long run, the choice is an individual matter that must be made on the basis of several distinct and equally important variables. These are reviewed below.

Patience, Impatience, and Temperament

If everyone in the world had the same personality, life would be terribly boring. The fact that we all have different perceptions of reality, in some cases, radically different perceptions, is the essence of creativity and the backbone of diversity. Perception and personality are to a large extent responsible for the existence of the securities and commodity markets. Different traders interpreting the same information in different ways is what makes for opinions, and opinions move markets.

Some traders are patient, methodical, premeditated, focused, and organized. They have the ability—whether inherited, acquired, or a combination of both—to sit and analyze markets, to enter orders, to wait patiently for their orders to be filled, and to hold a position as dictated by their system(s). Such traders are more suited to trade for longer periods of time. Hence, they have chosen position trading as their preferred method. Provided they can remain disciplined and organized, they will fare well as futures traders in the long run.

Other traders are anxious. They have limited patience, limited tolerance, and limited organizational skills. They react quickly and prefer to enter and exit their trades based on very short-term changes in market trends. Provided such individuals can remain disciplined and committed to a particular system or method, they can do well as futures traders in the long run and perhaps even in the short run. But in order to achieve even the slightest degree of consistent success, the day trader will need to follow a set or rules that may, at times, run contrary to his or her impetuous nature.

A third category of traders is positioned somewhere within the extremes of the position trader and the day trader. I term this category the "short-term trader." In most cases the short-term trader will hold a position for several days but rarely for only 1 day (unless a trade is closed out at a stop loss). I have already discussed the topic of short-term trading in my book *Short-Term Trading in Futures*.

Personality Traits of the Successful Day Trader

Your personality could very well be the key to whether you succeed or fail as a day trader. While you may make light of my claim, I urge you to take me seriously. If you have never day traded before and if you think that trader psychology has little to do with success as a day trader, then you have a lot to learn. My goal in writing this book is to help you avoid reinventing the wheel. Please take me seriously.

What are the psychological traits that contribute to success as a day trader? Based on my extensive experiences as a trader and as an observer of other day traders, I consider the following traits to either facilitate success as a day trader and/or to contribute to it:

- *Decisiveness.* This is by far the greatest personality trait a day trader can possess. Since day trading often requires split-second decisions, the day trader who hesitates is lost. Hesitation can occur either when placing an order to enter a trade or when placing an order to exit a trade. No matter when it occurs, it has destructive potential. Therefore, if you are not able to make a decision and act upon it promptly, you would do well to develop this trait if you plan to succeed as a day trader.

- *Persistence.* A day trader must have persistence. The successful day trader will not allow a string of losses to adversely affect his or her decisions. Rather, the day trader who wants to succeed will follow his or her trading system or method undaunted by a series of losses. We know from system testing and development that even the most potentially profitable trading systems will lose money 5 or even 10 times in a row before a profitable trade is hit. Day trading is no different. Therefore, the day trader who seeks success must have the mental discipline to avoid the insecurity that comes with a series of losses.

- *Confidence.* Closely related to persistence and decisiveness is confidence in the trading system or method. The successful day trader must believe that the system he or she is using will be profitable if it is applied with consistency and discipline. While confidence in self and system is clearly a quality that all traders should possess or develop, it is particularly important for the day trader.

- *Imperviousness.* To a given extent, a day trader must be able to resist the temptation of news and the opinions of other traders.

Day trading is a lonely game. You will need to maintain your composure while all those around you are losing their heads. In order to filter out the "noise," the day trader will need to develop a number of procedures—at times mechanical, at times psychological—to close off the potentially deleterious impact of news and inputs that are extraneous to the system he or she is using. This would not be the case for day traders who use the news as their method of trading. None of the methods described in this book depend on the news for their efficacy or signals. Hence, my advice is that you develop or amplify upon your ability to shut off inputs that may negatively impact your trading. Note that being impervious relates not only to market inputs but also to personal events in your life that may affect your trading.

Should you get some distressing news from home, should you have a disagreement with your mate or spouse, or should you have some emotionally evocative news about friends, family, or business, my advice is either to deal with it after the markets have closed, or if you are unable to shut off the impact of the event or events, to immediately exit your day trade positions.

■ *Contrarian attitude.* One step beyond being impervious is the ability and willingness to be a contrarian. The profitable opportunities in day trading often present themselves when it seems least likely that they will work. The profitable day trader may often have to buck the prevailing sentiment—selling when it seems that the entire world wants to buy and buying when it seems that the whole world wants to sell. If your trading system or method signals a buy when the market is plunging, then you must buy. If your trading system signals a sell when the market is soaring ever higher, then you must sell. Acting contrary to prevailing public and trader sentiment can only be achieved if you adopt and maintain a contrarian attitude to market opinions.

■ *Aggressiveness.* The marginally successful day trader will need to be somewhat aggressive, impervious, contrary, confident, and decisive. Developing these qualities and applying them consistently to the markets will likely bring you success if your trading methodologies have merit. However, the truly successful, highly profitable day trader will need to be highly aggressive. By this I do not mean that you will need to bust heads or curse at your broker. It does mean, however, that you will need to do the following:

- Pursue your broker relentlessly if you are waiting for confirmation of an order execution.
- Pursue your broker vehemently if an order has been missed, misplaced, or incorrectly executed by the broker, the floor trader, or other employees of the firm.
- Demand honest and reasonable price executions on market orders.
- Be willing to diversify into several markets, trading all at the same time if necessary.
- Maximize your results once you have learned to trade and once you have proof that your systems or methods work. In order to maximize your results, you will have to trade larger positions, thereby taking more risk for more potential profit.

- *Self-Control.* To a given extent, self-control in your trading is very much a function and a combination of all other qualities that I am discussing in this section. Being decisive and persistent, as well as having confidence in oneself and in one's system, are highly important in maintaining the self-control required for effective day trading. But I stress here that self-control is very important, since it is this quality that will prevent you from deviating from your system and/or from placing orders willy-nilly based on feelings rather than on facts. While feelings are important in relationships, the lack of feelings is important in trading.

The Dangers of Being Meek

The second-to-last trait discussed above, aggressiveness, is perhaps one of the most important for the day trader. Please understand that there is a significant difference between being aggressive in the sense of hostility and aggression to your friends, family, or acquaintances, and being assertive in the markets. Although the Bible may be right in stating that the "meek shall inherit the earth," the fact is that the meek will never be profitable day traders. It is entirely possible that the meek can develop into profitable short-term or position traders, but I suspect that they will never have what it takes to succeed as a day trader. In order to make day trading a profitable venture, you will need to spot trading opportunities quickly, you will need to identify them as actual opportunities, you will need to act on them immediately (but only if they're bona fide signals), and you will need to exit them promptly when your system so indicates.

And I give you another warning here: Be assertive with your broker or order-taker. Far too many traders believe that brokers are all-knowing. The fact is that your opinion may be better than your broker's opinion. Remember that the broker is *your* employee. The broker works for *you*. The broker is there to take orders from you. You pay the broker's salary for this service. And the broker must do as you say unless what you have told the broker to do is technically incorrect (i.e., placing an order that is inconsistent or not permitted). Therefore, you must be assertive with your broker when you place an order. Don't say softly to your broker, "Hi, this is Joe, remember me? Account 44578? Do you think you'd be willing to buy one June S&P contract at the market for me?" Don't ever do anything like that! Instead, place your order with confidence and assertiveness. Say "Joe, for account 44578, put one June S&P at the market." How you place your order and how you relate to your broker is a very important part of day trading (and this is true for position trading as well).

Finally, remember that as a day trader you must be immune to the persuasive powers of your broker. Remember that you alone are the best person to pass judgment on the validity of a day trade. You are the one who has (hopefully) researched your system. You alone are the one who has studied your system. And it's your own money that's at stake in the markets. Therefore, you must not under any circumstances allow your broker to talk you into or out of a trade. Too many traders believe that their broker knows more about the markets than they do. This may, in fact, be true. However, unless you play your own game and unless you call your own shots as a day trader, you won't learn anything about the game.

A Few Thoughts about Self-Control

Underlying all of the above is the very important quality of self-control. As I noted earlier, self-control is mediated and shaped by all of the qualities I've cited above. But self-control is not only important in placing orders and in following a trading strategy or system, it is also important in resisting the urge to overtrade. Some traders confuse overtrading with self-confidence and/or assertiveness. The fact is that trading too many positions and/or trading too large a position can undo you as quickly as can a lack of consistency or self-confidence. In order to preserve your self-control as a trader, I suggest that you regularly ask yourself the following questions:

- Am I trading only based on signals from my system(s)?
- Am I getting into trades based on actual signals or upon my anticipation of signals?
- Am I trading too large a position?
- Am I trading too many markets at the same time?
- Am I adding to my positions without systems signals?
- Am I reacting to news rather than to signals from my system?

Some Additional Thoughts About Day Trader Psychology

Clearly, the task of the day trader is more demanding than the task of the position trader. There is risk in all types of futures trading. The main difference is that everything that occurs within the time frame of a day is more intense than what takes place over a period of many days. Because decisions must be made on an instantaneous basis, the pressure on the day trader is greater than the pressure on the position trader. Therefore, if you plan to day trade, be certain that you are prepared for the increased pressures and the increased level of intensity.

Perhaps the single most important aspect of any trading methodology, whether for the long-term, intermediate-term, short-term, or day trade, is the psychology of the trader. My work with trader psychology dates back to the first trade I ever made in 1968. Having been trained as a clinical psychologist, and having practiced as such for quite a few years, I am very familiar with the limitations of the trader and with the psychological roadblocks that traders constantly throw in their own paths.

My book *The Investor's Quotient* (Wiley, New York, 1980) has continued to be a best-seller through the years, indicating not necessarily that my writing skills are tremendous, but rather that traders realize their limitations and seek to know more about how to overcome them. There are those who will disagree with me, but I feel strongly that this chapter is possibly the most important one in the entire book. While many of you may choose to either ignore what I have said in this chapter or skip it entirely, I do sincerely believe that to do so would be the worst mistake you can make. Although it is impossible to completely discuss in one chapter what takes several books to explain thoroughly, I will do my best to acquaint you with the pitfalls that await you as a day trader.

Day traders are in the unique position of having a very short-term relationship with the market. For many years day trading has been considered to be the most speculative of speculative trading activities. I believe that this is a market myth that has been perpetuated by those who are unable to day trade or who are afraid to do so. The fact is that the day trader is in an advantageous position. The true day trader understands the limitations of what can be achieved within the day time frame. The day trader is, therefore, the sharpshooter of futures trading. The day trader is interested in finding the most promising target, taking aim at it, pulling the trigger, and bagging the prey. That's what day trading is all about.

The day trader must be consistent, efficient, adaptable, and persistent. These are the most important qualities that a day trader can develop. Because day trading is unique among the many different avenues that are open to futures traders, day trading has its unique brand of psychology. In this chapter I will attempt to acquaint you with the major issues that face the day trader and, moreover, to suggest to you methods that may be used to overcome your limitations and to maximize your strong points.

A Successful Day Trader Needs Discipline

Before we examine the psychological and behavioral issues that limit success in day trading, let's examine the qualities that facilitate or enhance day-trading results. The first among these is discipline. Certainly by now you've heard the word *discipline* hundreds if not thousands of times. It is probably one of the most worn out terms in all futures trading. The problem is that merely saying the word is one thing; understanding its true definition operationally or on a behavioral level is far more important.

You can see, therefore, that discipline consists of many different things. Discipline is not any one particular skill. Perhaps the best way to understand trading discipline is to examine some of its component behaviors. Let's look at a few of these.

Persistence

This is, perhaps, the single most important of all qualities that a trader can possess. Day trading, and for that matter all futures trading, is an endeavor that requires the ability to continue trading even when results have not been good. Because of the nature of markets and trading systems, bad times are frequently followed by good times, and good times are frequently followed by bad. *Some of a trader's greatest successes will occur following a string of losses.* This is why it is extremely important for traders to be persistent in applying their trading methods and to continue using them for a reasonable period.

Those who quit too soon will not be in the markets when their systems begin to work; those who quit too late will run out of trading capital. Therefore, while persistence is important, it is also important to know when a trader has been too patient when it is time to quit and not play any longer using the system that you have been using.

If persistence is so important, then how does the trader develop it? The answer is simple, but the implementation is not. Persistence is developed by being persistent. Although this may sound to you like a circular answer, it is truly not. The only way to be persistent is to force yourself initially to do everything that must be done according to the dictates of your systems or method. Try this, if you're having difficulty: Make a commitment to a trading system or method. Follow through with that approach for a specific amount of time, taking every trade according to the rules or, if the system is subjective, attempting to trade the system with as much consistency as possible.

If you have been consistent in applying your rules, then you will find that, in most cases, your consistency will have paid off, and you will have profits to show for your efforts. Even if your trading was not successful, you will have learned a great deal. You will have learned that you can follow a system or method, that you can trade in a disciplined fashion, and, moreover, that the only way to do so is to be persistent by following as many of the trades and rules as possible.

Compare this to the ignorance and confusion that comes from haphazard trading or by applying trading rules inconsistently. Think back to your experiences as a trader. Remember your worst losing trades. You will find that *those losses that have been taken according to a system or method are easier to accept psychologically, whereas those that have not been accepted according to the rules have often turned into terrible monsters, ultimately costing you much, much more than they should have, financially as well as psychologically.* If you would like to master the skill of persistence, then you will need to practice it. Make the commitment and I think you will see some wonderful results, even over the short term.

Willingness to Accept Losses

Here is yet another important quality that the effective day trader must either possess, acquire, or develop. Perhaps the single greatest downfall of all traders is the inability to take a loss when it should be taken. Losses have a nasty habit of becoming worse rather than better. Unless they are taken when they should be, the results will not be to your liking.

Although it is easier for the day trader to take a loss than it is for the position trader (since a loss must be accepted by the end of the trading day), it is still the downfall of many a day trader who is unwilling to accept the loss when it is a reasonable one. The good day trader must have the ability to take a loss when the time to take that loss is right. What's right is dictated by the particular trading system or risk management technique that is being used. I would venture to say from my experience and observations *that perhaps 75 percent or more of all large losses occur because losses were not taken when they were small or relatively small or when they should have been taken.*

I can certainly speak from experience when I say that my largest loss ever resulted from the fact that *I refused to take the loss* when the time was right. I allowed a $500 loss to turn into a $5000 loss. Fortunately, that was the first and last time I was guilty of that serious a transgression. Unfortunately, many traders, a great many traders in fact, refuse to take losses when the time is right. Fortunately, the day trader has two opportunities to take a loss. *The first one is at the stop loss point as determined by a system or at the predetermined dollar risk stop. The second point is at the end of the day.* A day trader is, therefore, fortunate inasmuch as he or she is forced to liquidate all positions at the end of the day. This will keep losses smaller than they would be if losing positions were carried overnight.

Here are some suggestions as to how you may improve your ability to take losses when they should be taken:

1. *Formulate your stop loss rules very specifically.* Do this whether they relate to systems or dollar risk amount, and type or write your rules in large print. Place the hard copy close to your quotation equipment, the computer that you use for trading, or the telephone from which you place your orders. If you do not use a computer or quotation system for your trades, then please keep your rule handy on an index card and refer to it frequently during the day.

2. *Make the commitment to accept your next 10 losses completely as dictated by your system.* Once you have done this, the behavior will become habitual and losses will be easier to accept.

3. *If you trade with a full-service broker or a trading partner, make your broker or partner aware of where your stop loss will be.* Have them remind you that you must exit your position accordingly. You may wish to give them the authority to do so for you, assuming of course, that your relationship with them is sufficiently close to allow for such a procedure.

4. *Place your stop loss.* A much more simple procedure, although I do not necessarily recommend it at all times because of the nature of day trading, is to actually place your stop loss as soon as your entry order has been filled.

These suggestions will, I feel, help you master the ability to take losses in a timely and rational fashion.

The Ability to Avoid Overtrading

Too many day traders feel that they must trade every day. Let's face it, some traders are addicted to trading. A day without a trade for them is like a day without a meal. The fact is that there are some days that offer few if any trading opportunities. *The day trader who wishes to preserve capital and avoid losses as well as unnecessary commission charges should understand that day trading is not an everyday event.* There will be days when no trades are indicated. Believe me when I tell you that things are better that way.

One of the telltale signs of the day trader about to go astray is the searching-for-a-good-trade syndrome. Have you ever found yourself sitting at the computer or quotation screen, bored because there have been no trades that day? Have you ever found your fingers idly rambling over the keyboard, searching chart after chart looking for markets to trade? *Yes, my friend, this is the first sign of trouble.* Should you ever find yourself in this position, *do yourself a favor and stop looking.* Good day-trading opportunities within the parameters I have set forth in this book are plentiful, but they do not occur every day. Consequently, set yourself standards as to which markets you will day trade, and if there are no day trades in these markets, do not allow yourself to endlessly wander about the keyboard looking for day trades in such things as orange juice or palladium. They may work for you from time to time, but the odds of success are very slim. Take my word for it, the successful day trader will specialize in only a handful of markets and will do well at these. Do not attempt to spread yourself too thin by looking for trading opportunities where in fact they do not exist. And this brings me to my next point.

The Ability to Specialize

Successful day trading is a time-consuming undertaking that requires close attention. In many cases it require diligence, follow-through, and persistence. Although some day-trading techniques I have discussed in this book, specifically the gap methods, lend themselves to strictly mechanical trading, many do not. It will be possible for you to enter orders for gap trades without watching the markets closely. However, the vast majority of techniques require close attention. Therefore, it is unfeasible for most day traders to be involved in too many markets at one time. I suggest that day trading three markets is sufficient for the majority of traders. In fact, for new day traders, I would recommend specializing in only one market, attending to this market thoroughly and carefully in order to develop your skills and to increase your overall profits.

What should the new day trader trade? Naturally, the answer to this question will change as a function of market conditions. Some markets historically have lent themselves well to day trading—the currencies, S&P futures, and Treasury bonds.

However, some markets such as silver, soybeans, the petroleum complex markets, and other currencies make good day-trading vehicles as well under certain market conditions. Consequently, I would pay attention to these as well when they become sufficiently active and volatile. In terms of gap trades, there are many markets that are good day-trading vehicles inasmuch as entry will be on a specifically defined buy or sell stop with exit usually on the close of trading. Since gap trades do not in many cases require close attention, many markets may be day traded in this fashion. For the newcomer, however, I would recommend a very limited portfolio of trades until techniques have been mastered and self-confidence has been achieved.

Beginning with Sufficient Capital

Perhaps one of the worst blunders that any trader could commit whether trading from the day time frame or from a position trade perspective is to attempt trading with insufficient capital. The argument may be made that the day trader does not need to have substantial capital in his or her account, since trades are closed out at the end of the day and therefore the necessity for sufficient margin to maintain positions is eliminated.

While this may be true, it is also true that those with limited funds cannot play the game as long as those with larger funds can. It is important in any venture to start with sufficient capital in order that the trader not feel pressured to perform and to allow the particular trading system or methods sufficient opportunity to ride through periods of poor performance.

The trader with limited capital will not only be a nervous trader, looking always to minimize losses beyond the point of realistic trading, but also will frequently be knocked out of the game after a series of losses, before his or her trading methods have had the opportunity to perform. Consequently, capitalize your trading account sufficiently or decide ahead of time that you will trade only a very limited portfolio consistent with your available capital. Do not start with an undercapitalized account, since this is a near-certain invitation to failure. In order to begin trading with sufficient capital, the aspiring trader will have to be realistic and, above all, patient enough to gather the speculative capital that will be needed.

The Ability to Use News to Your Advantage

Many a trader has learned the hard way that following the news can frequently lead to losses. I have discovered that there are ways in which the trader may use the fundamental news or developing international, domestic, or political news to his or her advantage. To use the news in your favor, *do not be a follower of the news, rather "fade" the news.* Use the news to exit positions that you have most likely established well before the news has become public knowledge. I am a firm believer in the old market dictum: buy on rumor, sell on news.

On an intraday basis, markets are very sensitive to news well before the news is known by most traders. Insiders buy and sell on expectation, sometimes based on rumor, frequently based on fact. They establish positions before the general public is aware of the news, and once the news has become public knowledge, they take advantage of the surge or the drop in prices to exit positions.

Therefore, if you wish to use the news to your advantage, you must be a contrarian. This is especially true from the day-trading perspective. Although there is nothing wrong with following intraday trends, frequently intraday trends react strongly to news developments. If you are following your trading system or method, you will most often be on the correct side of the market when such news develops. Take advantage of price surges or declines to exit your position. This requires self-control and the ability to see the news as your opportunity to get out, not as your opportunity to hold on for even more profit!

Taking Advantage of Brief Price Surges

In order to day trade profitably, you must also learn to take advantage of brief flurries in prices. In the previous section I discussed large intraday price moves that can occur in relation to international, domestic, political, and economic news. At times, markets will drop or rally quickly seemingly in response to no news. What may be happening in such cases is that is a rumor on the trading floor, a large buyer or buy order, or large seller or sell order of which you are not aware. Such brief price surges or drops are opportunities for you to exit positions consistent with the price move.

Regardless of the source, consider all price rallies or declines that occur quickly within the day's trading session to be an opportunity for you to either exit your current position at a profit, or to establish a new position using support and resistance methods that have been outlined previously. Developing this quality as a day trader is important, since it is entirely consistent with the day-trading objective. Too many day traders assume that bulges or sharp declines in price within the day are basically meaningless. Believe me, they're not. They're tailor-made for the day trader. The day trader who is committed to taking a profit out of the market every day must take advantage of these price moves. If you decide not to do so, then by all means you must either raise or lower your stop loss (depending on your position), or you must use an appropriate mental stop loss, which is adjusted to the change in price. What this means simply is use a trailing stop loss in the event that the price move is negated shortly after it begins. In this way you will have given yourself an opportunity to lock in a larger profit that you might not otherwise have had.

Sticking to Your Daily Goal

Above all, remember that as a day trader you have one major goal and that is to make money trading each day. The important consideration here is that in order to make money day trading every day, you will need to be particularly aware of your net profits during the day (after costs) and as the day progresses if you are riding profits. You will be more inclined to take those profits in order to make each day profitable.

My advice, which is based on many years of short-term and day trading, is to set yourself specific standards regarding when you will begin to liquidate positions toward the end of the day in order to guarantee yourself a profitable day. My advice is to do so approximately 1 hour before the close of trading. You may either begin to close out your positions at that time or you may use a follow-up stop loss procedure in order to "lock in" existing profits.

Many traders would disagree with my advice. As I indicated earlier, however, it is based on many years of trading experience, and it is designed to achieve a very important goal for the day trader. As a day trader you need to end each day with a profit, no matter how small that profit may be. If you can do so, you will be reinforced positively for your day-trading skills. This will give you confidence and a positive attitude toward your trading profession, which, of course, is very important, particularly when you have experienced a string of losses. In other words, if you can be even slightly successful each day, your attitude toward day trading will become more positive, your self-confidence will increase, and you will be more able to withstand the temporary reversal to which all traders, short-term, long-term, and day traders alike frequently fall victim.

But in order to achieve this goal you will need to internalize it, keeping it foremost in your mind at all times. What is right and proper for the position trader or for the short-term trader is not necessarily good for the day trader. If you find yourself wanting to ride profits or losses overnight, then you are not being true to your goal as a day trader. Should you wish to day trade and position trade as well, then I urge you to do so in different accounts in order to avoid the confusion that will assuredly come from doing both in the same account. Keep your goal in mind, and you will be less likely to stray from it.

Using Market Sentiment to Find Day-Trading Opportunities

I have already discussed the importance of going against the majority opinion in order to find profitable day-trading opportunities. *I believe that this is one of the most important qualities a day trader can possess.* While there is certainly a great deal of money to be made day trading with the existing trend, *it is also important to know when the existing trend has reached a possible turning point.* One of the best ways, if not the best way, of doing this is through the use of market sentiment.

Since I have already discussed the particulars of applying market sentiment for the purposes of day trading, I will not repeat this information here; however, I do again stress its importance. *The day trader must also be a contrarian.* This does not mean that you must buck the trend, but *it does mean that you must always be aware of whether sentiment is very high or very low.* This will give you important clues as to whether you should be quick to take profits, whether you can allow profits to run, and whether you should look for trading opportunities on the opposite side of the existing trend.

Summary

Although there are many other important qualities that a successful day trader must either possess or acquire, I believe I have covered the most significant ones. If you strive to develop these qualities, *then your odds of success as a day trader will certainly be better.* I have learned, after my many years of trading, that *the major difference between those who are successful traders and those who are not is to be found in their psychological make-up and in the skills they have acquired as traders rather than in the trading systems they use.*

Although it is certainly helpful to have an effective trading system, even the best trading system in the hands of an undisciplined trader is nothing more than a destructive tool. Consequently, you must develop your skills as a day trader along the guidelines I have given you in this chapter.

Occasionally, traders will have idiosyncratic difficulties in the markets that must be addressed on an individual basis. If this is the case, then I suggest you identify your particular problem as succinctly as you can, and if you cannot formulate a good method for minimizing the problems that this behavior causes you, I suggest you contact a professional for assistance. If you are not successful in your search for help, please drop me a line and I may have some helpful suggestions for you (MBH Commodity Advisors, Inc., P.O. Box 353, Winnetka, IL 60093).

16
The Day Trader's
Rules for Success

I had an aunt in Yucatan
Who bought a python from a man
And kept it for a pet
She died, because she never knew
These simple little rules and few
The snake is living yet.   HILAIRE BELLOC

Day traders are no different in their unwillingness to follow rules than are most traders. The good news is that if the day trader fails to follow the rules of successful trading, his or her end will come swiftly and decisively. The consequences will be quick and the lesson will be a definitive one. There will be very little waiting or wondering. Why is this good news? I say it's good news because when you break the rules of profitable day trading you'll get your feedback promptly. And this will give you an opportunity to change and to learn, provided you want to. The position trader, on the other hand, may often need to wait many weeks or even months before he or she realizes that a faux pas has been committed. And this will slow the learning process significantly.

It is impossible for me to overemphasize the fact that consistently profitable traders, and in particular, consistently profitable day traders, are great because they have mastered the discipline of trading as well as the necessary and reliable mechanical aspects of day trading. Throughout this book I have emphasized the great importance of self-discipline as a trader. Clearly, the weakest link in the chain of trading is the trader. There can be no consistent success without a mastery of self and self-discipline. There are many opinions as to what constitutes discipline. And there are many different opinions as to how one may undertake the often arduous and self-effacing task of acquiring self-discipline.

Different traders, different writers, and different behavioral analysts will give you distinctly different opinions, all based in part on their observations and experiences. But take care if you heed any advice you are given by someone who has never traded. Unless the individual who is giving you assistance is a professional psychologist, counselor, or behavioral therapist, take all points of view and all directions of assistance with a few grains of salt.

Know that the following suggestions and observations have been tempered and shaped by nearly 30 years of trading, market analysis, research, and observation. My trading has exposed me to every conceivable type of market and every conceivable type of news event. My trading has taken me to the highest of emotional highs and the lowest of emotional lows. I have been on all sides of the trading fence. I have broken practically every rule in the book, and I have even broken rules that were not in the book. My own losses and failures have forced me to develop an arsenal of time-tested methods, attitudes, opinions, and procedures, which I now share with you. The best way for me to convey this information is by listing, not necessarily in order of importance, what I have discovered.

Determine Your Orientation— Know Your Direction

One of the most important things a day trader can do is to arrive at a comfortable and confident place in terms of system, method, procedure, and orientation. It is important for the trader to find his or her place in the ever-growing world of day-trading possibilities. What markets should you trade? What systems or indicators should you use? What quotation system or data feed should you use? How often should you trade? Should you be a "scalper" or should you take things more slowly? Should you give up your job to trade full-time or should you wait and take things slowly?

There are many things a day trader can do, but only a limited number of them can be done at the same time. Using the information presented in this book and in *The Compleat Day Trader*, find one or several techniques that make sense to you. Try them out on paper or on a modest basis in real time until you feel confident with them. These will be the techniques you should use in your trading.

Once you have chosen your methods, use them consistently, day in and day out, whenever you have a signal or a trade. Make a commitment to trade the signals strictly by the rules for a certain amount of time, for a given number of trades, or for a given amount of risk capital.

You will find that certain techniques work best in certain markets: S&P futures, for example, are especially well suited to the many of the systems I have described earlier. However, you may not feel comfortable with S&P futures. T-bond futures are particularly well suited to the support and resistance, scalping-type methods I have discussed. Currency futures, given their sharp and fairly quick moves, are especially well suited to hit-and-run trading methods and/or to some of the spread indicators contained in this book. The gap methods I have presented herein also work well in currencies but with some variation on the theme. Determine which approaches suit you best and devote your time to those methods consistently and for a reasonable period. Find your place and rest in it for a while. Learn from your mistakes and from your visceral and emotional reactions. Make every loss count. Losses are your tuition.

Don't Be Surprised If You Lose Money at First—Some People May Never Succeed

Many traders are disappointed and frustrated when immediate success in day trading isn't forthcoming. I urge you to persevere. Be persistent in giving yourself sufficient time to achieve success. We know from our evaluation of trading systems and methods that even the best system can lose money 7 or 8 or even 10 times in a row. It is the nature of the trading beast to bite you a few times before you show a profit.

Learning day trading from a book is like learning how to ride a bicycle by reading a book. Once you try to do it on your own, you have to be prepared for a few falls. But with care, precautions, and consistency you'll avoid breaking your neck when you fall.

Even if you have more than a slight amount of experience in position trading, you may still find yourself initially losing as a day trader. Although you may feel that your position-trading experience will serve you well, it may actually prove detrimental, since you have approached day trading with preconceived notions that may stand in your way, clouding issues and confounding your thinking. You will need to abandon these dysfunctional ideas in favor of those that I have offered in this book, if what I've said makes sense to you. Remember that this process takes time. Some failures at first are unavoidable. You will need to fall off the bicycle a few times before you can ride it. At first your riding will be shaky and slow. After a while, however, you will feel at home on the day-trading bicycle, and it will take you where you choose to go, provided you follow a smooth road.

How long will it take you to become a successful day trader? There is no answer other than perhaps more than 2 weeks and less than 2 years, perhaps never; however, these are certainly not hard-and-fast rules. Some of you will become successful day traders in several weeks, whereas others will never achieve consistent success.

Expect the Least, Not the Most

There are too many books on positive mental attitude that tell you to have great expectations. They tell you to visualize success. They encourage you to engage in affirmations. They push you to see yourself as a highly profitable trader or investor. I take issue with all of these books, and I caution you against having unrealistic expectations. Try not to have great expectations. Expect to lose. Expect that with time you should begin to break even. Expect that with more time and with more experience you will begin to show profitable results.

Do not expect profits at first. Rather, expect that learning the game will cost you tuition both in terms of time and money. Therefore, you must understand the reasons for your every loss and you must learn from them. There are hundreds if not thousands of traders who begin their trading with unrealistic expectations, a few thousand dollars in risk capital, and a total lack of discipline or method. They soon leave the markets beaten, broke, and broken. In the meantime, their money has been gobbled up by professional traders who thrive on the losses of tyros. If you have any expectation, then expect failure while hoping that through your learning experiences you can minimize the failures and maximize the successes.

Shut Out the Input of Others—Play Your Game by Your Own Rules

Should you allow yourself to be exposed to, pandered to, and intimately influenced by the many fantastic claims for perfect trading systems and "Holy Grail" seminars, then you will be diverted on your road to success. There is nothing wrong with attempting to improve on what you are doing, but the act of endless searching will distract you from your goal. Don't get sidetracked on your journey. If you are confident with your trading methods and rules, then use them and profit by them. Persevere and ignore the claims and opinions of others as much as you can.

Those who purport to have better systems, better methods, foolproof indicators, outstanding results, and fail-safe risk management will constantly barrage traders with their claims. Before you give any of these serious attention, make sure that what you're doing is not better. Every system you test, every seminar you attend, every piece of software you buy, and every path you take may prove to be a costly excursion away from your final destination. Each takes time, effort, and money. And these are the most precious commodities in the world. They are limited resources not easily replaced.

Therefore, I suggest you find a methodology and commit to it for a predetermined length of time. And during this period of time do not allow yourself to become distracted by anything else, even if it means that you need to close your eyes and ears to the magazines, newspapers, and mail you receive.

Take Your Losses When Your Signals So Dictate— Don't Make Excuses!

Riding losses is the worst thing a trader can do. Not taking a loss when you should take the loss is the worst thing you could do. I have stated repeatedly throughout this book that the single worst offense a day trader can commit is to carry a position beyond the end of the trading day, particularly if it is a losing trade. At times a profitable trade carried overnight may become even more profitable on the next opening. This issue has already been discussed objectively as the FPO exit (first profitable opening) and the nth profitable exit. But a losing trade usually gets worse if not closed out. *If you fail to exit a trade at the end of the day, then you are violating the essence of day trading and you therefore risk exposure to everything that a day trader seeks to avoid. Do not, under any circumstances violate this cardinal rule regardless of what the excuse or excuses may be.*

But what if you are locked into a position due to a limit move against you? In such an event you have no choice but to carry your position. You could spread a position off (take an opposite position in a different contract month if possible) in order to avoid the exposure; however, there is still danger, even in a spread. Remember that you are either a day trader or you are not a day trader. There is nothing wrong if you choose not to be a day trader. But note that you must not change horses in midstream, since this will, in the long run, cause you losses. In the short run, you may be very pleased with the results. But in time, your lack of discipline will haunt you.

In the event of a limit move in your favor, you may be tempted to hold your position overnight, expecting that there will be more profits in the morning. Even this is a dangerous procedure because a limit move in either direction on any given day does not necessarily guarantee follow-through in the same direction on the next day. You will note from some of my research in the preceding chapters that holding a day trade until the nth profitable opening may in certain very specific circumstances prove more profitable on than exiting on the close of the day. But note that these are very specific conditions that are related to the day-trading systems and indicators being used.

My research has shown that over the next several days there may be follow-through; however, what happens between now and then may wipe you out. I have already given you certain very specific conditions under which a day trade may be kept overnight, but beyond these suggestions, I emphasize once again that a day trade must be closed out by the end of the day unless there is statistical evidence to support carrying the trade overnight or to the nth profitable opening.

Your Goals as a Day Trader

Your first goal every day of your life as a day trader is to end the day with a profit. Place no dollar amount on the profit. To set a goal too high would be unrealistic and to set a goal too low might be aiming too low. Another type of goal—the goal of following your rules and being true to your methods—is the major goal of the day trader. However, if you do need to establish a goal for yourself in terms of dollars, then try to end each day with a small profit at the very minimum. As a secondary goal, you should attempt to follow all your rules and methods. In fact, your goal of ending each day with a profit will not be possible unless you have been true to your systems and methods.

Don't Exit Trades Too Soon

Too many traders exit their profits too soon. Note that the historical results and statistics on the indicators and systems presented in this book are based on exit at the end of the trading day or on a trailing stop loss. To exit trades before the system or method so dictates is to violate the rules that I have presented to you. All too often you will exit a trade based on a whim, a hunch, a fear, a concern, or a news item, and you will be very sorry later that you did so. A good trade is a good trade. Do not exit a profitable day trade either until the end of the day or unless your trailing stop loss is triggered according to the rules. I cannot stress this too strongly.

At times you will want to exit a trade, but you will follow the rules and avoid the temptation. At the end of the day you will realize that breaking the rules would have resulted in a large profit. Instead, you followed the rules and took a small profit. This is the nature of the markets. For every one time that you break the rules, at least twice as often you will find that following the rules would have been more profitable.

Furthermore, not following the rules teaches you nothing. Every time you break a rule you will have a different excuse. The only thing that breaking the rules will teach you is to break the rules. As a result, your trading will deteriorate and you will quickly become one of the thousands of undisciplined traders who inhabit the vast wasteland of losses.

Don't Hold a Profitable Day Trade
Beyond Its Ideal Exit Point

Many a good day trade has become a bad day trade, turning from a profit into a loss, because of poor intraday risk management or to the tenacity of the trader. Holding on to a winning trade beyond its exit point (i.e., trailing stop loss) can also get you into trouble. Please remember the rules I have given you about trailing stops based on the systems presented herein. This is an important rule that you must not violate. Preservation of capital is quintessential to consistent success as a day trader, and preservation of profits is equally as important. The mere fact that a trade looks too good to exit is just as much a violation of the rules as is exiting a trade because it looks bad. Remember that "looking good" or "looking bad" are subjective and intuitive responses that have no place in the repertoire of a day trader unless that day trader is a bona fide psychic with a proven track record of trading success.

Don't "Force" Day Trades If
There Are No Signals

Many traders have the personality type that thrives on action and withers on inaction This fatal flaw causes them to search out trading opportunities where none exist. If you have day-trading signals but find yourself anxiously searching through your screens and intraday charts for trading opportunities, then you're headed for a disaster. If you find yourself looking at markets that you never trade for opportunities that you have not seen previously in the day, then you are most likely headed for trouble. Do not attempt to create an opportunity where one does not exist. Be patient. There will be trades tomorrow or the next day. The market always provides opportunities over time even though none may exist today. Don't ever, ever force yourself to trade if an opportunity does not exist.

One excellent way to overcome this problem is to use a software program such as TradeStation™, FutureSource™, Commodity Quote Graphics™, MetaStock™ or Aspen Graphics™. These trading software programs will gather your intraday data for you and, once set up with your parameters and/or signals, alert you to trading opportunities. If there are no signals, then there are no trades. You will save time and errors, and you will improve your trading discipline by using such programs. I highly recommend them.

Hesitate and You Lose!

Hesitation is one of the worst enemies of the day trader. The age-old expression "he who hesitates has lost" is truer in the futures markets than in any other venture other than life-and-death situations. Since day trading occurs within a circumscribed period of time, every moment you lose in entering or exiting a position is a moment that may cost you money.

If you choose to hesitate, then do so with premeditation and calculated caution. *Never allow yourself to hesitate out of fear or indecision.* Hesitation subsequent to a clear trading signal or opportunity indicates a lack of confidence, and a lack of confidence indicates that you are not comfortable with your choice of systems and/or methods or with your skills as a day trader. Hesitation can be costly. Fortunately, you will know that you are hesitating the instant you do so. Use this as a trigger to let yourself know that you are about to make a potentially expensive error.

Keep a Record of Your Trades—the Good, the Bad, and the Ugly

I pointed out earlier in this book—in fact, I noted a number of times—that every loss you take is an important learning experience. But a loss can be of no value unless you know why you took the loss and what you will do in the future to avoid making the same mistake. Clearly not all losses are a result of breaking rules. Many losses are a simple result of your system being wrong. But you must know when your system was wrong and when *you* were wrong. There is a significant difference between the two.

Therefore, I urge you to keep a log or a diary of your trades, noting each trade with a brief commentary as to whether the trade was a profit or a loss due to following your system or due to breaking your rules. A profit that resulted from breaking your rules will teach you something wrong. A loss that has occurred as a result of breaking your rules may be very instructive. A diary should not only be kept, but it should also be referred to both at the end of each trading day and at the beginning of the new day. Refer to everything you did the day before and learn from it.

Don't Day Trade Unless
You're Properly Informed

Some of the techniques I have discussed in this book are almost entirely mechanical. In order to trade them, your presence is not required and live price quotes are unnecessary. In most cases a broker can actually do the trades for you, depending upon the ground rules and understandings you have established with that broker. Other methods, however, require your presence and close attention. If a situation arises during the day that requires you to leave your quote system, then either close out your positions immediately or give your broker stop close only or market-on-close orders. *Do not attempt to keep in touch with the markets by calling frequently for quotes or by using a portable quotation system. This is not a good way to operate.*

And this brings me to the question of whether a trader should attempt to trade when on vacation or when separated from his or her quotation system or computer. Clearly, my reply is no, unless you have a partner or broker who can follow the trades for you.

When in Doubt, Stay Out

The old expression "when in doubt, stay out" is especially appropriate for the day trader. Not all indicators or signals will be completely clear all the time. Furthermore, some other developments such as news, reports, or short-term fundamentals make signals unclear or market response uncertain. In such cases my best advice is to stay out; do not trade. There will always be plenty of trades, and there is no need to enter a trade unless its potential outcome is relatively clear and free from the erratic influence of news or other fundamental events.

You Can't Succeed Unless
You Do Your Homework

I have found few traders who are consistent and conscientious about doing their market homework. All too often they slip into the abyss of laziness in the hope that they have somehow internalized their system rules. But the fact is that they expect to show a profit without having to work for it. There can be no success with a system unless you follow the system. And you can't follow the system unless you perform the necessary daily calculations or procedures.

It never ceases to amaze me how few traders consistently do their market homework. Even though they have developed good market indicators and effective trading techniques, they fail to consistently keep up-to-date on the markets and allow a good methodology to turn into a bad one by virtue of their laziness. This makes no sense to me whatsoever. The fact is that if you develop something that works, and if it is making money for you or facilitating your ability to make money, then by all means you ought to continue with it. Too many traders become complacent about their market studies, fail to do their homework, and then wonder why they lose money. If you intend to succeed, then you must do your homework no matter how simple or complex it may be.

Perhaps you have developed a trading system that requires no homework. This is certainly possible. A number of the techniques described in this book do not require homework. However, you will still need to work on your trading diary, and you will still need to keep in close touch with trading opportunities that may develop during the next trading day. The only way to do this is to study the markets. This is what I mean by homework, and this is why it must be done.

Keep Close Track of Your Results

Some traders refuse to monitor their trading results as a form of defense against being distressed by bad results. This is neurotic behavior, and you should not engage in it. It will cost you money. Know where you stand and keep in touch with your results, always comparing them to what your systems should ideally be generating. Always keep close track of your results on a trade-by-trade and day-by-day basis. If you know how your systems are performing, you will have effective and valuable feedback about the techniques you're using.

Unless you know your trading results, you will not have sufficient information about how well or how poorly your methods are performing. I suggest you use one of the many computerized accounting programs to keep track of your results, or at the very minimum, a spreadsheet that is updated manually will certainly do the job. Pay especially close attention to your average winning trade and your average losing trade. Your average winners should be consistently larger than your average losers. If they are not, then you are risking too much and getting too little for your efforts. This is an indication that change is necessary.

Another good reason for keeping track of all your trades and their results is to determine if and when your trading technique, system, or indicators have deteriorated and are in need of change or review. Unless you check your performance, you will not be cognizant that change is necessary, other than perhaps a vague feeling that all is not going well.

More Complicated Is Not Synonymous with More Profitable

There is no doubt that you will be tempted many times to use more complicated trading systems. You will be tempted to build more and more rules into your system, feeling, erroneously, that your system will work better if it has more rules. You may feel that if your system takes more market variables into consideration, you will trade more profitably. My experience strongly suggests otherwise. With the exception of artificial intelligence-based systems that can process vast amounts of data in exceedingly complex ways by relating data to market patterns and relationships, adding new inputs or variables to your own analytical techniques does not necessarily improve them and may in fact cause them to deteriorate.

I have found that if there is a relationship between complexity of system and profitability of system, then it may well be an inverse relationship. The simpler a system is, the more likely it is to be profitable. So, please, don't confuse apparent complexity with profitability.

The Danger of Market Myths

Be careful what you believe. Be careful whom you believe. Be careful what you read. Be careful who influences you. The markets are forever subject to the emotional influence of traders. Through the years traders have come to believe that certain relationships exist in the markets when in fact these relationships do not exist at all. Statistically, few consistent market relationships have persisted over many years. Therefore, be careful not to get caught up in the cycle of hope that perpetuates market myths.

In this respect, you must also be careful about the information you allow to filter into your unconscious mind. The lure of fantastic claims and outstanding new discoveries about trading will always be there to play with your insecure side. Don't give in to any of these claims. If your systems are making you money, then don't look for greener pastures. This does not mean that you cannot or should not engage in ongoing research. But remember that there is a big difference between productive and objective research and emotional response to a claim. Should you be attracted by a claim, a system, or a promising indicator, test it before you use it.

The Dangers of Pyramiding

Pyramiding is the act of adding increasingly larger units to your position as a market moves in your favor. Therefore, you may begin by buying one unit and adding two additional units once the trade has moved in your favor. If the trade continues to move in your favor, you may add four new units, and then, assuming that it continues in your favor, you might add six or eight units. The upside of this methodology is that you will accumulate a very large position consistent with the trend and you will use the capital available in open profits to margin new positions.

The danger of pyramiding is that this is a pyramid clearly built upside down. It is heaviest at the top and rests on only one unit at the bottom. It is therefore subject to violent collapse at the slightest indication of a trend reversal. If you intend to build a pyramid, then do so by establishing your largest position first and follow it up by successively smaller numbers of units.

Avoid Inactive Markets

I have already given you guidelines on which markets to day trade and how to determine if a market should be day traded. Follow those rules. By trading active markets only, you will avoid the problems that come with thinly traded markets and the relatively poor price executions that are so common in such markets. As a day trader, you must have liquidity in order to move into and out of your positions easily and without too much slippage. Moreover, if you intend to trade large positions, then liquidity is absolutely essential for success. As a day trader, you do not have the time to wait too long for price executions to be reported to you, nor will you have the time to go back and forth with different price orders in an effort to have your positions either entered or closed out.

Since markets wax and wane in terms of trading activity, you will need to evaluate this on an ongoing basis in order to make certain that you are participating in actively traded markets. If you find yourself trading thin markets and experiencing all the difficulties that go along with such markets, then I assure you that you have no one to blame but yourself, since you have violated one of the cardinal rules of day trading.

As this book is being written, the active futures markets are as follows: S&P 500, Treasury bonds, Swiss franc, Deutsche mark, yen, British pound, crude oil, and heating oil. Coffee has spurts of activity. Some of the European markets also make good day-trading vehicles. As you can see, the number of vehicles open to the day trader is rather small. But this, I assure you, is a blessing in disguise.

Don't Run with the Lemmings

Some of the largest intraday moves occur when they are least expected. The general trading public and a vast majority of professionals will be on the wrong side of the market when these moves happen simply because they get blindsided by their collective lemming instincts. Mob psychology is a very important factor that may be used to the advantage of the day trader. If you find that the market sentiment is skewed to one side of the market or another, then watch closely for timing indicators that will give you market entry on the opposite side of majority opinion.

Watch for Day-Trading Opportunities Following Major Events or News

Many outstanding day-trading opportunities occur on the heels of a major news event such as a political upset, a financial panic, unexpected news, natural disasters, the threat or actuality of armed conflict, or other emotion-provoking news. When these events occur, the markets are highly emotional, and opportunities for the disciplined day trader abound.

The Value of Correct and Timely Price Data

Some traders will attempt to save money by subscribing to delayed price quotes or to low-cost real-time quotes. My advice: don't do it. Day trading is difficult enough with good data. Why decrease your odds of success by using incorrect data or delayed price quotations?

A Few Thoughts about Commissions and Brokers

Traders have a choice of dealing with either full-service or discount brokers. The price difference between dealing with a full-service broker and a discount broker can be significant. But so can the service. If you're an experienced trader who is skilled at order placement and who is trading a system that does not require immediate reporting back of price executions, then a discount broker will suit your purposes well. However, if you're a newcomer to trading and if you require instruction, hand-holding, and coaching, then the additional service you'll get from a full-service broker may be well worth your while. Once you have learned your lessons well, you can graduate to a discount broker if you like. Note also that some discount brokers are not particularly prompt in reporting your price executions to you. Some of the systems presented herein require you to know where you have been filled so that you may place your stop loss, training stop loss, or reversing stop. In such cases you will need to make certain that your broker, whether discount or full-service, understands the importance of reporting your price executions to you promptly. In most cases, trading only active markets will minimize the delay in reporting order fills.

While these are just a few of the important rules to remember when you trade, they are by no means the only prerequisites to success. Develop and maintain your own list or rules. Your list should be based on your own experiences as a day trader, since your personal list will be more meaningful to you. The rules I have give you are merely a beginning, a base upon which I suggest you build and expand.

Summary

This chapter highlighted the rules I consider important for success as a day trader. While you may disagree with some of my rules at first, I can assure you that in the long run you will come around to my way of thinking and doing. You may want to keep a list of your own rules as your experience with day trading develops. Note that the rules in this chapter have been gleaned not only from years of experience in trading but also from the observation of other traders. Every loss you take as a trader is an expensive lesson from which much can be learned. However, in the absence of attention and study, nothing will be learned from your losses and there will be no progress. Success can often teach you as well; however, as in the case of failure, lack of attention to the reason(s) for your success will mean that valuable information has been lost or not recognized.

17
FAQs

(Frequently Asked Questions)

In much wisdom is much grief: and he that
increaseth knowledge increaseth sorrow.
ECCLESIASTES 1:18

What Equipment Will I Need
to Day Trade?

The type of equipment, software, and price quotations you will need are a function of the trading methods you have selected. All of the methods that I have discussed in this book that require either 10-minute, 20-minute, or 30-minute data will require you to have a live, tick-by-tick data feed as well as a computer and software to process the data and indicators. I have often been asked if delayed data can be used. My answer is a categorical and emphatic no. To day trade with delayed data is to begin with a handicap. For the relatively small amount of money you will save by using delayed data, the limitations you will experience will not be worthwhile.

I have also been asked if data delivered via Internet is acceptable. My answer is yes, as long as the time delay is not significant. The longer the lag behind the data that comes off the trading floor, the less likely your chances of success. It's that simple. So if you'd like to begin day trading with your best foot forward, do it right and get live data that is not delayed. There are a number of vendors who provide such data. Note that unless you plan to trade on all of the exchanges or in all of the markets, you won't need to buy live data for all markets. And this could save you a considerable amount of money.

Several excellent software programs are available for processing the tick-by-tick data. You will need to do some homework in order to find out which one of them is best for you. Costs can vary considerably, so take your time and decide. Some software vendors offer a free trial period. Take advantage of it. This is an important and often expensive decision, so please don't take it lightly. The computer hardware you'll need depends on the software you buy, so make that decision last, not first, unless you plan to buy a top of the line high-speed computer that is loaded with memory and disk space.

What Methods or Systems Should I Use?

The systems or methods you will use in day trading should be chosen by you, not by me. Only you know how much you can risk, how attentive you can be to the markets, how you relate to different systems, and how much discipline you have. So take your time before you decide what method or methods to trade. Evaluate them. Watch them in real time. Paper-trade them for a while if you like. Take a test-drive and trade them briefly in real time. Then decide what works best for you.

Wouldn't It Be Best to Trade the Most Accurate Systems?

Accuracy is not nearly as important as most traders believe it to be. More important than accuracy are drawdown, maximum consecutive losing trades, and average profit or loss per trade. If your system has reasonably low drawdown, a small number of consecutive losers, and a high average profit per trade, then the accuracy won't matter too much. Trading systems with a low accuracy rate can make money if the average profit per trade is high and if the risk is managed effectively. As a rule of thumb, try to avoid systems that have an accuracy rate of less than 55 percent. Note that there are many systems whose accuracy falls in the 40 percent to 54 percent range that have shown excellent overall profits with large average profit per trade.

There is nothing wrong with such systems provided you have the discipline to follow them. They will lose more often than they win, but when they win they'll win big for you. Just remember that one of the things that causes a trader to lose his or her discipline is a string of losing trades. Low-accuracy systems tend to have long strings of losing trades. And this will test the resolve and discipline of even the best traders. Be forewarned! You may be better off trading a system that has a relatively small average profit per trade but high accuracy than a system that has a large profit per trade but relatively low accuracy. A lot depends on your personality and temperament.

I've Heard Traders Say that 90 Percent of Their Profits Are Made on 10 Percent of Their Trades—What Exactly Does This Mean?

This is one of the most profound statements you will encounter in the futures markets. Understand it, internalize it, and believe it. I'll explain it to you as succinctly as I can. The simple fact of life that characterizes all commodity trading is that about 90 percent of all trades will eventually balance themselves out as neutral. After subtracting commissions, slippage, small winners, small losers, large losers, and medium-sized winners, the net result, or bottom line, will often be zero.

What's left will be 10 percent of the trades whose sum total must be profitable if the overall outcome of your trading is to be positive. It would, of course, be preferable if the 10 percent of trades consisted of large profits. This is what ultimately makes the difference between winners and losers. Winning traders are able to amass a certain number of highly profitable trades. But these trades are in the minority. They will nevertheless prove to be the backbone of the system.

In back-testing trading systems we find that most systems base their success on only a relatively few large winning trades each year. It is important, therefore, that the position trader or the day trader ride each winning trade to its maximum potential or its ideal exit point as determined by the system that is being used. To exit too early may cut your profits short. The idea is to cut your losses short while maximizing your profit.

How Much Money Do I Need to Begin Day Trading?

Here is a case in which more is clearly better. The less money you begin with, the less likely you are to be profitable. The reasons are simple to understand. If you begin with $3000 and you lose $1000 three times in a row, you are out of the game. It is not unusual to lose three times in a row. In fact, it is usual to lose three times in a row or more. Even losing on seven day trades in a row would be fairly typical.

In addition, you must also make certain that you have sufficient margin money for the markets you want to trade. While some brokers will allow you to day trade with relatively little capital in your account, most brokers want to protect themselves from potentially uncollectable customer deficits and will therefore require you to have enough money in your account.

Finally, the amount of money you will need to get started will also depend on how volatile the markets are. The more volatile a market, the more money you will need to have, since the price swings and potential losses will be fairly large. There is, therefore, no quick and easy answer to the question of how much money you need in order to get started. The only thing I ask you to be certain of is that you do not lower your odds of success by starting with a small amount of capital.

Can I Realistically Compete with the Floor Traders When I Day Trade?

I do not believe that most day traders compete with the trading floor. Pit brokers do not do the same thing we are trying to do. Their trading is, for the most part, based on scalping, or shaving a tick or two off trades as often as possible each trading day. Since floor traders pay very small commissions, they can make a profit on one tick in many markets. Those of us who trade off the floor can't do that. Therefore, we do not compete with the typical floor trader.

There are floor traders who attempt to extract larger moves than a few ticks within the day time frame. I do not consider them competition either. They tend not to use the same types of systems that we are using. Many do not trade based on a system but rather on their "read" or intuitive sense of the markets. They judge the direction of a market based on their sense of what the trading floor or large traders are doing, on the source of large orders, or on the reaction of the pit to news and events. This is not to say that there are no systems traders on the floor. There are. But I do not believe that their aggregate trading is sufficient to overcome the power of thousands of off-the-floor day traders.

Why Can't I Hold a Trade Overnight If I'm a Day Trader?

Note that I am not telling you can't hold a trade overnight. I'm merely saying that if you do, then by definition it is not a day trade, and you therefore open yourself to the potentially negative influence of events and developments that could adversely affect your positions. I am also not representing that carrying a trade overnight is always a losing proposition. I have demonstrated in this book that some of the systems I have developed actually perform better if carried overnight. But remember that in addition to the exposure of holding a position overnight, the result may be a margin call due to the increased margin you will have to post since your positions will have been carried overnight.

How Many Markets Can I Realistically Trade in One Day?

With the assistance of a computer quote system, you can track many markets during a day. Realistically, however, you may only be able to trade seven different markets a day. If you trade the markets actively, then you'll know that only a handful of markets can actually be day traded given volume and volatility. There may only be from four to six markets that are worth day trading.

How Flexible Can I Be in Following Your Systems?

Many years ago I would have told you that being flexible is important. Today I know differently. I suggest that once you have researched my systems and once you have worked with them to see how you fit them and how they fit you, be as inflexible as possible in following the systems. If there are any rules you *must not break* they are the rules governing risk management. Take your losses when your system tells you to do so.

Can I Enter a Market with One System and Exit with Another?

Some traders like to combine systems. I do not consider this good practice. A system is a system because its performance is based on a set of rules generated specifically for the conditions and markets that were tested. To combine one system with another, picking and choosing entries and exits based on each system, is not recommended. If you trade a system, then trade that system to the exclusion of all else.

Do I Have to Trade Every Day?

No. Fortunately, the markets provide many opportunities during each week. You do not need to trade every day if, for instance, you trade on the same weekday or weekdays. Some systems and indicators seem to have a day-of-week effect. S&P futures, for example, tend to close higher on Mondays. Buy signals on Mondays in S&P tend, therefore, to be more accurate. By trading on the same day or days of the week you will be able to take advantage of such day-of-week effects where they exist.

Should I Pyramid My Day-Trading Positions?

Pyramiding can be very profitable or can be the tomb of ruin. All too often traders add larger and larger numbers of contracts to their original position, thereby raising their average cost. When the market makes a small move against them, their profit is gone. A heavily pyramided position can turn from being profitable to being a big loser very quickly. Whether a pyramid will work for you or against you depends on how you build it. The tendency is to begin with one contract, then add 3 more, 5 more, 10 more, and so on. The result is a top-heavy pyramid that can come crashing down. To profit using a pyramid you must be a good builder. Take your largest position at the beginning, then add successively smaller units as the market continues to move in your favor. You might begin with five contracts, then add three, then two, then one.

Should I Attempt to Get Flash Fills on All of My Trades?

A *flash fill* is a price fill that occurs within seconds of the trader placing an order. Once the order is placed, it is called down to the trading floor when it is signaled to the pit broker by hand. The pit broker reports back the fill by hand signal, and the client is notified. The whole process can take from as little as 1 minute to as long as 3 minutes. It is a highly efficient and very prompt way of getting market orders executed. Where such fills are possible, use them.

How Do I Know When to Increase the Number of Contracts I Trade?

There is no hard-and-fast answer to this question. While some professional traders will give you a formula by which you may determine when to begin trading larger positions, I do not believe that the formula approach is best. What's more important than a formula is your own sense of comfort. Some traders can feel very comfortable trading 20 S&P contracts at a time, while others balk at even one contract. But remember that confidence in trading can't be the only variable. False confidence and overconfidence can both be invitations to failure in day trading (or, in fact, in all forms of trading). In order to be successful in trading more than one contract and more than one market, you will need to evaluate your success as well as your desire (or lack thereof) to trade multiple contracts. I know of no concise formula for doing this.

Should I Consider the News or Fundamentals in My Day Trading?

If you're a technical trader, then you must ignore the news. The news can often lead good traders astray. But the news can also be your friend by providing you with excellent entry and exit points for your trades. A very bearish piece of news followed by a technical buy signal is an important event. The news says one thing, but the market says another—and the market usually wins. If you use the news, then do so for the purpose of taking positions opposite from the news based on your methods. Obsessing about the news, about reports, or about anticipated events is not part of technical day trading.

How Can I Stop My Broker from Talking Me out of or into Trades?

It's a sad but true fact that traders are all too often insecure about their day trades (and all other trades as well). They allow themselves to be talked out of and into trades. But the fault is not that of the broker. The responsibility belongs entirely with the trader. Naturally the trader will attempt to blame the broker. This is often unfair. The best way to avoid such problems is to establish an understanding with your broker from the start. Tell your broker that you only want advice when you ask for it. Tell your broker that you will close your account if the rules you establish at the outset are violated.

Some of you may decide to work directly with a broker. In such cases the above would not apply. However, remember that if you work with a broker and if you respect the broker, then you must follow what the broker tells you. But remember that you can just as easily subvert what your broker tells you as you can subvert what your system tells you. Without discipline and follow-through nothing is possible.

Afterword

A Few Closing Words about my Work

Now that you have read my words and familiarized yourself with my work, I feel it is important to bring a few very important issues to your attention. I address these points for a dual purpose. First, I think it's important for you to understand why I trade, why I publish, and why I research the markets as I do. And second, it is important for me to defend, in advance, any criticism that may be directed at this book, its ideas, its efforts, and its concepts.

Why I Do This

There are several things that have prompted me to write this book. First and foremost, I feel that day trading is here to stay. Given the international situation and interrelationships of all world economies, the effects of a price change in London, Hong Kong, or Singapore will have a substantial effect on markets in the United States and vice versa. This has been a growing trend since the early 1970s. It is important for the trader to know how to deal with such situations and, moreover, how to take financial advantage of them.

As the speed of communications continues to increase, substantial market moves will likely occur in shorter and shorter time frames. Speculators will continue to add to market volatility. The result will be an even greater increase in short-term and day trading by professionals and the public. Hence, it behooves all traders to learn some valid methods for day trading.

Yet another reason I have written this book is to dispel some of the popular myths and methods that are currently considered valid as day-trading approaches. I do not mean to imply that the methods and systems discussed in this book are the best methods, nor do I mean to imply that they are the only methods; however, I do believe that have merit. If you are currently a day trader, then examine some of my ideas. They are based not only on a considerable amount of experience but on a vast amount of research as well. It is unfortunate that so many traders are willing to accept market myth and conjecture as market fact. Accordingly, I have attempted to differentiate between the two, indicating what still needs to be thoroughly tested and what has already been tested. Hopefully, my work will help steer you away from what is specious and toward what is reasonably factual.

In addition to the above, still another reason for my having written this book is to direct traders to the study of market patterns as a viable approach to day trading. The current trend toward complex trading systems driven by a plethora of inputs is, I feel, counterproductive, inasmuch as it does not reflect reality. While it may be true that the best day-trading systems will ultimately be those that can recognize and evaluate a large number of inputs and market-related factors, the current state of computerized trading technology is not yet at the point where this is a reality. Although considerable advances have been made in the areas of artificial intelligence (AI) and neural networks (NN), I see very little hard evidence to support the application of such methods to day trading or even position trading. Note that I am not discarding such approaches. In fact, I believe that they are indeed the wave of the future. But we are not there as yet. I also feel that effective AI models for day trading will be heavily based on market patterns. Hence, some of the patterns in this book should be seriously considered by traders as potential inputs for AI trading models.

Should you wish to pursue day-trading system development, then I suggest you do so using AI-based models. However, be aware that the critical variable in all AI and NN systems is the learning model or "brain." If the learning paradigm is faulty or not capable of evaluating market variables, then the output will be useless or worse. Do not confuse the success of AI and NN models in industry with what can be achieved in the markets. What works on an assembly line will not necessarily work in the markets, where trader emotion and a host of random events must be considered as valid market inputs.

My last major point in this synopsis relates to public and professional reaction to this book. Having achieved some degree of name recognition and notoriety given my more than 30 books on trading and my 30 years as a trader, market analyst, author, public speaker, educator, and writer, there are those within the futures industry who take pleasure in attacking my ideas because they do not coincide with their market orientation. I have taken great care in this book to avoid throwing stones at any system, method, or indicator. I have maintained a purely objective approach, citing statistical research where I have it and differentiating opinion from fact where necessary. Hopefully, my work will not offend anyone. However, I am a realist. I know that, for one reason or another, there will be those who take issue with what I have said, with what I have discovered, with how I have applied it, with how I have written it, with how I have taught it, or with how I have suggested you apply it.

There will be those, for instance, who say I have overly optimized my results. To them I say that this is not the case. In fact, I have intentionally understated the results of my work so as to avoid giving anyone a false sense of what is possible. Some of the systems I have developed have shown a historical accuracy of over 80 percent with large average profits per trade as back-tested. I have not included these, since I feel that to do so would be too flamboyant. Furthermore, I feel that such back-test results were achieved by heavy optimization and would likely be unattainable in real time. To those who feel I have optimized my results too heavily I also say that the systems included herein contain nothing more than the standard variables that are known to be important inputs for any system. These are as follows:

- A method of entry selection
- A risk management stop loss
- A method of exit selection
- A method for trailing stop losses once a given profit has been achieved

The methods I have shared with you are all based on logical concepts and have strong face validity. They are therefore reality-based, testable, operational, and subjective. I have been careful to point out that few systems or methods will have a static set of indicators over time. As markets change, day traders must adjust their systems to such changes. And such changes will always be a function of market volatility. A fixed $500 stop loss will suffice in a relatively quiet market; however, it will be an invitation to destruction in a volatile market. Accordingly, I have encouraged you to be flexible in trading your systems, and I have given you some historical records to show you how differing degrees of market volatility require different degrees of risk as well as adjustments in timing signals. But the underlying concepts are what I stress. In other words, if you understand the concepts of my methods ands indicators, you will find it relatively simple to adjust the actual length of timing variables and the size of stop losses to the inherent characteristics of the markets.

And then there will be those who take issue with my insistence that day trading is a viable method for today's times. Know that I am being very clear when I state that day trading is not right for all traders. In fact, there are many aspiring traders as well as newcomers to trading who have no business trading and who, from the outset, are destined for failure. In order to overcome the notion that day trading is right for everyone or that trading is right for everyone, I have included my extensive writings on trader psychology, discipline, trader behavior, and the art versus the science of trading. Read them carefully if you haven't already done so.

Finally, there will be traders who are angry with me because they applied some of my principles and lost money with them. In most cases such losses are the fault of the trader and not the method. The trader who can follow a system or method thoroughly is a rare trader indeed. The trader who claims to have lost money following a system will, upon being questioned, admit that the system was not followed consistently. Traders will break rules no matter how specifically the rules have been stated and no matter how many times they have been warned not to break the rules. While I cannot guarantee that the methods and systems presented in this book will continue to be profitable, I do feel that the underlying concepts are valid and will withstand the test of time. The intelligent trader will take my ideas and adapt them to current markets and conditions. The undisciplined trader will subvert and pervert my ideas, using them willy-nilly, whimsically, and inconsistently. And I have no control over such abuses.

Although I have done my best to be specific in this book, presenting you with concise rules and methods, I urge you to do your own work in going forward with my methods. The search for cookbook trading methods will never end. Traders will always seek such approaches. While there is much to be said in favor of such mechanical methods, there is also much to be said in favor of adapting your system or method to current market conditions and to markets where they may perform optimally. I have discussed this above and in previous chapters. Please consider my comments seriously before you trade.

Perhaps I have spent too much time defending my position against potential attack or in cautioning you against the abuse of my ideas and systems. But I do so because I feel that since your hard-earned money is at stake, you will appreciate my cautions. Day trading is not as difficult as some would have you believe, but it is also not as simple as others would have you believe. To be successful at the fastest game in town, you will need to be consistent, adaptable to changing market conditions, strict in managing risk, unemotional, and open to new ideas.

It's Time to Take Flight

My work is now done. I have given you systems, methods, indicators, analyses, rules, observations, insights, and understandings. The rest is up to you. Armed with my information and your understandings, and equipped with sufficient starting capital, accurate price quotations, a good working relationship with a broker, and motivation, you're now ready to either step out on your own for the first time, or you are prepared to step back into the trading arena more confident, more protected, and more educated.

You can use what I have taught you, or you can integrate my tools into your trading style. I don't claim to have all the answers, and I don't give you any guarantees other than to tell you that with persistence, patience, and motivation you will succeed. If I can help you on the road to success as a day trader or if I can clarify any of the information presented herein, then please don't hesitate to contact me. You may wish to contact my Internet Web site at *http://www.trade-futures.com* for more information and updates on my work.

I have learned enough about the markets in my more than 30 years of trading to know that the more I learn, the more there is to learn. And I also know more than ever before that what has worked best for me is that which is both the most simple to do and the most simple to understand. I have shared this knowledge with you in the hope that it can help you as well. If my writing, research, and observations can improve your results or change your point of view for the better, then I will have done my job and I will be happy.

Jake Bernstein

Index

Index

About the Author

Jake Bernstein is an internationally recognized author, trader, and researcher. He publishes the *MBH Weekly* commodity letter and, as the author of some 30 books and research studies, Bernstein's influence and renown stretch across the globe. He has been a guest on *Wall Street Week* and scores of other radio and television programs, and is a popular speaker at investing and trading seminars.